First-Person Preaching

First-Person Preaching
Bringing New Life to Biblical Stories

Daniel L. Buttry

Judson Press ® Valley Forge

First-Person Preaching: Bringing New Life to Biblical Stories
© 1998 Judson Press, Valley Forge, PA 19482-0851

Library of Congress Cataloging-in-Publication Data
Buttry, Daniel.
    First-person preaching : bringing new life to biblical stories / Daniel L. Buttry.
    p. cm.
    ISBN 0-8170-1275-3 (pbk. : alk. paper)
    1. Biographical preaching. 2. Monologue sermons. 3. Sermons, American.
4. Baptists—Sermons. I. Title.
    BV4235.B56B88 1998
    251—dc21   97-53070

Printed in the U.S.A.
06 05 04 03 02 01 00 99 98
5 4 3 2 1

To Sharon A. Buttry,
Harriet A. Buttry,
and the late Lucas W. Buttry,
three preachers whose
lives and faith
have molded the life and faith
of this preacher

Contents

Acknowledgments

Every book, while perhaps having only one author's name on the cover, is the product of many people. This book is no exception.

First I must thank the people of Dorchester Temple Baptist Church in Boston, Massachusetts, and First Baptist Church in Dearborn, Michigan. They may say that they have been taught and inspired by my preaching, but I have been taught and inspired by them as their preacher.

In producing the manuscript, making copies, and dealing with the computer, I have received gracious assistance from Dian Cullens and Susan Smith. Sharon Buttry and Emmett Johnson read the manuscript, caught numerous errors, and made suggestions that improved the book when I was wise enough to take them.

As always, I have appreciated working with the staff at Judson Press, particularly Kristy Arnesen Pullen and Victoria McGoey. Their competence and affirmation are an author's delight.

Finally, I acknowledge the great cloud of witnesses, dead and living, who have shaped me as a disciple of Christ: Harriet and Luke Buttry, Francena Arnold, Sharon Buttry, Bob Webber, Gordon Fee, Ka Tong Gaw, Arthur Rupperecht, Jimmy and Gale Hull, Tom Preston, Rich Thompson, C. S. Lewis, Dietrich Bonhoeffer, Kathy Vignoli and Jack Melvin, Brother Lawrence, Scott Heald, Bill and Paulea Mooney-McCoy, Roger and Claire Dewey, George Williamson, Ken Sehested, Glen Stassen, Madeleine L'Engle, Martin Luther King Jr., Stuart Hackett, David and Jean Wolfe, Bill Hyer, Steve Seibert, Christie Calao, April Baker and Deborah Lynn, Emmett Johnson, Paul Nichols, Carole Dieciedue, Bob Tiller, Carol Pierskalla, Stephen Charles Mott, George Lakey, and Saboi Jum.

Each of these people, along with others unnamed, has influenced

me in ways I can specifically identify, ways that have made me a
better person. There is no way that their contribution could *not* come
out in my preaching or writing. A preacher can preach only out of
who he or she is by the grace of God. Each person from this cloud
of witnesses has been a channel of that grace, and I carry their gifts
with me as I minister.

Introduction

There is power in the story. My father was a preacher. The two sermons of his that I remember best were both stories. "The Courage of Onesimus" related the story of the runaway slave who became a Christian under the apostle Paul's ministry. Onesimus went back to his former master, Philemon, carrying a letter in which the apostle exhorted Philemon to receive the young man "not now as a servant, but above a servant, a brother beloved" (Philemon 16, KJV—Dad preached from the King James). The drama of the risk taken by Onesimus in that return made a challenging story of faith.

Dad's other sermon came out of the story of Jesus' passion. "Testimony of a Military Serviceman" was based on the words uttered by the Roman centurion upon the death of Jesus. Dad, a military officer himself, an Air Force chaplain, wove together the actions of the Roman soldiers from the trial before Pilate through the crucifixion to the empty tomb, telling the greatest drama through a smaller actor. Dad used the mundane paperwork of an officer as the vehicle through which God's holy drama was delivered.

Dad did not assume the character of the central figures in these sermons, but he used his imagination to weave a consistent and compelling tapestry of character and narrative. Onesimus and the centurion came alive to me. I felt their dilemmas and grappled with their choices. These stories became favorites in the congregation, sermons that could bear repeating. All of us in the family can recall the main themes of these sermons, for the story form carried them deep into our memory.

When I was in the Soviet Union in 1988, I had the opportunity to preach in a Methodist church with five minutes' warning. Amid the excitement of being in "enemy country" during the astounding transitions of the days of *perestroika* and *glasnost,* I had no time to prepare what I might say. So I went deep into my memory to the story-sermon I had heard as a child. The sermon was very different from Dad's, but he would have recognized it. As I told that congregation the story of Onesimus and his courageous decisions in the face of an uncertain future, their own reality was placed before God's eternal word. I preached an echo from that remembered sermon: "We don't know what the future holds, but we know who holds the future." "Amen!" responded the congregation, for which I needed no translation.

This story had been heard from a pulpit in childhood but was powerful enough to sink into memory and emerge again at a moment's notice when the need arose. This book is about telling stories in a particular way so that the old, old story becomes vivid and alive for a new generation of hearers. It is about taking strange names and making them into familiar, living presences. It is about opening a door of imagination through which the Holy Spirit can guide us into new discoveries of God's revelation. It is about telling others' ancient stories so that God's story can become our story.

So, my sister and brother readers, I invite you to take in these stories. Let them live in you. Discover other stories throughout the Bible and live in them. Allow the characters to open their thoughts and feelings to you. Let the Spirit shine a light on the movement of God in the drama of these characters. Then preach the tale in your own special way as God's storyteller. You will stand in the great line of those who have passed on that story from generation to generation to generation.

PART ONE

Preaching in the First Person

CHAPTER ONE

Story in the Bible

For many people in the church the first exposure to the Bible comes when they are children in Sunday school. In that setting we are told the stories of Adam and Eve in the garden of Eden, Noah and the ark, David and Goliath, baby Jesus born in a manger, Jesus feeding the five thousand and walking on the water. We don't learn theology per se in that Sunday school class; rather the theology lies deep within the stories that fill the Old and New Testaments.

The Gospels, the scriptural centerpiece for our Christian faith, are mainly stories. Stories *about* Jesus are told as well as stories *by* Jesus. Jesus' own teaching was frequently done in parables: he related tales of a father and his two sons, a woman seeking justice from an unjust judge, a labor dispute over wages, a shepherd seeking a lost sheep, a farmer scattering seed in hope of a crop, a wealthy man building bigger barns for his growing hoard, a woman cleaning house in search of a precious coin. Jesus told stories that came out of the experiences of the people around him. Yet his parables were also layered with meaning, so he would offer them with the admonition, "Let anyone with ears to hear listen!" (Mark 4:9).

Many Bible scholars hold that the Gospel of Mark itself is based primarily on the stories related through the preaching of the apostle Peter. John Mark, according to tradition, accompanied Peter and took note of the stories about Jesus in the preaching of the apostle.

The rich details of an eyewitness, such as those of Jesus sleeping on a cushion in the storm-tossed boat (Mark 4:38), make the stories in Mark's Gospel the most vivid we have of Jesus. Mark put portions of Peter's oral message down in writing, weaving them into a coherent larger story and eventually reaching us with the life-giving Good News.

The God revealed in the Bible is a God who acts in human history. God calls Abram and Sarai to leave Ur and act on a promise. God delivers Joseph from prison and lifts him to the heights of power in Egypt. God hears the cries of the Hebrew slaves in Egypt and sends Moses to lead them from their bondage. God parts the Red Sea so that the Hebrew people can cross to safety; then God closes the sea upon Pharaoh's army. God has Samuel anoint David as king of Israel. God judges the kingdoms of Israel and Judah for their idolatry and injustice, sending them into exile. God brings back the remnant peoples from Babylon to rebuild Jerusalem.

This is "salvation history," *Heilsgeschichte,* and it is full of stories. God is revealed in concrete action with specific human beings amid the flow of historical events. Christians and Jews proclaim a God who is not just a theological and philosophical object of thought and analysis. God is a subject, an actor, *The Actor* in history. Salvation is a drama played out on the stage of the world with acts that span the length of time. Human beings like us have their parts to play, parts that often reflect the complexity of their character, but the star is the living God who acts and calls people to act in this drama.

For Christians the Incarnation is the ultimate story. God in Christ takes human form, joins us on the stage not just as the divine, overarching presence but as the human actor subject to the same temptations and limitations with which the rest of the human cast must live. The third act in a Shakespeare play is always the hinge act, the crisis in the drama to which the earlier acts build and from which the rest of the story inevitably unwinds. The Incarnation is the central moment, that hinge act, of the salvation-history drama. Jesus is born, lives, teaches, heals, is crucified, and rises again. We know so well the stories of Christ's story. The church year is built around the twin celebrations of Christmas and Holy Week, the

beginning and the climax of the Incarnation story. Everything prior
to the Incarnation event has built up to this point of the drama;
everything that follows will be understood in the light of that pivotal
event.

Though there was, and still is, much thought and discussion about
the meaning of the Incarnation event, at the core of our gospel
presentation is not the analysis but the story. Mark's Gospel, probably
the first of those written down, is the most story-filled of the four
Gospels in the Bible. Mark starts simply: "The beginning of the
gospel of Jesus Christ, the Son of God" (Mark 1:1, RSV). The Good
News, the literal meaning of *gospel,* is at its core a story. The Good
News is not primarily theological propositions to which one gives
assent. It is a story that captures us with its central figure. We are
called to enter that story, to make our story part of Christ's story.
Even that primary theologian of the early church, the apostle Paul,
wrote about his gospel as, at its core, a story:

> Now I would remind you, brothers and sisters, of the good
> news that I proclaimed to you, which you in turn received, in
> which also you stand, through which also you are being saved,
> if you hold firmly to the message that I proclaimed to you—un-
> less you have come to believe in vain.
>
> For I handed on to you as of first importance what I in turn
> had received: that Christ died for our sins in accordance with the
> scriptures, and that he was buried, and that he was raised on the
> third day in accordance with the scriptures, and that he appeared
> to Cephas, then to the twelve. Then he appeared to more than
> five hundred brothers and sisters at one time, most of whom are
> still alive, though some have died. Then he appeared to James,
> then to all the apostles. Last of all, as to one untimely born, he
> appeared also to me. (1 Corinthians 15:1-8)

To convey our faith adequately, then, we as preachers must tell
the story. The story of salvation history says more than any of our
analytical schools could say. The story of the Good News speaks
deeper to the human heart than any of our theological principles.
The story comes alive for us again and again so that the vast sweep
of millennia is spanned through an immediacy of divine and human
contact. We can identify with Abram and Sarai and Hagar. We can

feel with Moses and Hannah and Jeremiah. We can relate to Mary and Martha and Peter. Through the Holy Spirit, God at work in their lives becomes a channel through which God can work in our lives.

CHAPTER TWO

The Power of Drama

Stories are important in our faith journey because their drama holds power. The drama of a good story can grasp the hearers and transform them. The drama has the power to stimulate feelings, thinking, and action. It then becomes the igniter of new drama, moving from the story of the tale to the story unfolding in the hearer's life.

Part of the power of drama lies in its concreteness. Abstract issues or principles can be analyzed and discussed on a theoretical level, but such discussions tend to remain in small circles of the intelligentsia. Sheer analysis or historical recounting can put people to sleep. But in a human drama, the issues become tangible. A discussion about the history of the Salem witch trials and mass hysteria may be fruitful and intellectually stimulating, but Arthur Miller's play *The Crucible* makes the witch trials a vivid, living reality. The characters of the play draw us into their lives and fears. The period and the people seem far more real to us when presented in the dramatic form than when we dispassionately read a dissertation.

Successful drama engages our feelings. When we witness a drama or hear a well-told story, we identify with some of the characters. Either their situations are close enough to the situations we face so that we step into their shoes, or something about the characters invites us to enter their skin and feel the tension of their dilemmas. We aren't engaged at merely a rational level; rather our fears, loves, hopes, anxieties, and joys are elicited. In the classic thriller *Wait until Dark,* Audrey Hepburn plays a blind woman trying to escape a killer in her house. After many tense episodes she seems to have killed her assailant, and the viewers in the theater start to relax. Suddenly a hand grabs her ankle, and a unified scream erupts from every throat in the theater. Our relief and our terror are at the raw edge because of the power of the story. Film and television writers know how to manipulate those feelings, to build up terror or pathos, to evoke a scream or a tear. They know the power of their medium.

The power of drama is such that lasting images are seared into our brains. A lecture about a historical event will be largely forgotten. Certainly the details will fade quickly. But a drama aids our memory, making even the details stand out clearly a long time later. I've known about the Dred Scott case as a shameful example of U.S. constitutional law during the pre–Civil War era, but I couldn't have told you much about it other than that the decision supported slavery. Then, while visiting the old courthouse in St. Louis where the case was tried, I participated with a number of other tourists in a dramatization of the landmark trial. I was one of the members of the jury. Though this play took place five years ago, I can easily recall details of the case and the various issues we weighed as we considered the merits of the two sides. The drama turned the case into living history. It became part of my memory through direct experience.

Many if not most of us think in pictures. When we are talking about a baseball game, we can see it in our minds; the image may be unclear, but it is there. When a friend is named, we picture the person. Drama connects to those images and builds on them. It creates new images that then have a life of their own in our memories.

We have all heard the proverb "A picture is worth a thousand words." Maybe no picture has captured the truth of this proverb as graphically as that of the lone Chinese man standing before a line of tanks near Tienanmen Square during the 1989 democratic uprising in Beijing. The drama of a frail, unarmed human being standing before such raw military might spoke volumes about courage, commitment, and risk. That photograph is on the cover of my book *Christian Peacemaking,* and I later had occasion to show it to a number of people in Burma, a nation under military rule. Though some of us could not communicate because their English was as lacking as my Burmese, their faces and intensity revealed their excitement as they viewed the photo of that man and the tanks. They could feel along with him. They were inspired in the face of the repressions they had to confront. The drama in a vivid picture had power to communicate more deeply than words.

Movies can speak to us with the same power when the drama and the image are artfully woven together. All of us probably can recall scenes from films we watched even decades ago. The power of their drama—of humor, romance, adventure, or horror—can still trigger the echo, often a powerful echo, of the initial experience. Even a seemingly remote event, such as the thirteenth-century wars between the Scots and the English, becomes a vivid inspiration for struggling for freedom in a movie like *Braveheart.*

Good drama provokes deep responses. Drama gets to the center of our being where action is generated most powerfully in our heart rather than in our mind. Our heart is the source of power. Our action can be guided by our mind, but without the heart those actions will be shallow, bland, and impotent. Whether in sports, art, love-making, singing, or preaching, the ones whose hearts are engaged will reach the highest levels possible for them, perhaps even exceeding the level of their skill through the power unleashed in the heart. Drama connects to that deeper core, eliciting the deeper response that can transform. A story can be told, and its memory can be recalled to reenergize one for the work inspired by that story.

CHAPTER THREE

Story and Drama in a Sermon

Preachers use story frequently in sermons. Many sermons are preached from biblical stories told in the third person. This form is very familiar to preachers and often is no more, in a literary sense, than an expansion and elaboration of the original story. We make our running commentary on the biblical text, drawing out the applications for the hearers. Most sermons on historical narratives in the Bible take this form.

Preachers also use stories as illustrations. A theological principle, no matter how profound, can be uninspiring to most listeners. So we use stories to make the theology breathe, to incarnate the principles in the experiences of ordinary life. We follow an excellent example. Jesus said, "The kingdom of God is like . . ." and then told a story. Sermons on the intellectual side are made memorable to the hearers either by alliteration or by illustrations, or by both. These techniques don't have to be cute tricks to manipulate; they are tools to aid in effective communication. The gospel needs to be clearly delivered to the minds and hearts of people, so effective communication tools serve a holy task.

Early Christian preachers also used stories in their sermons. Stephen in Acts 7 told the salvation story of the people of Israel, culminating in Jesus Christ. Stephen reflects the recitation of the salvation history found in the Psalms (see, for example, Psalms 78, 105, 106, and 136), liturgical expressions of the faith community that continually rooted the Israelites in their national story. Paul repeatedly told the story of meeting the risen Christ on the road to Damascus. His own account of his preaching in 1 Corinthians 15 emphasizes the passion of Jesus and the resurrection accounts.

Many sermons in the early church were given in the first person because the preachers were characters in the drama of salvation history. Peter's sermons, on which Mark's Gospel may have been based, were full of Jesus as seen through the apostle's eyes. Peter could tell of his own direct experiences—his steps of faith and his acts of foolishness and fear. He could paint the pictures for his hearers' imagination with details etched in his own memory. Peter used drama just by being himself. So how would I as the modern preacher tell the story if I were Peter? Through vivid imagination I can re-create for my hearers that initial telling of the story. The immediacy of the event was Peter's, but it now belongs to all of us.

Re-creating that immediacy is a challenge for the contemporary preacher. We can draw some help from the field of drama.

A number of actors have modeled the powerful use of solo dramatic speech with few if any props. I'll never forget the first one-person drama I saw. It was about a priest in nineteenth-century Hawaii who lived among the lepers. The actor shifted from character to character, and the narration opened new perspectives on the main figure. The actor brought us inside the skin of each of the characters as his "I-language" compelled our identification.

A preacher of first-person sermons does the same thing, but with a gospel twist. We bring a story of good news, a message of salvation, liberation, and healing. The drama we present is a small part of God's bigger drama. The dramatic sermon concretizes the good news. In the first-person sermon we take one of the characters from the Bible, or perhaps church history, and bring the person to life, just as the actor of the one-person drama brings a chosen character to life. We live with the characters. We sense their hopes, feel their dilemmas, reach out with them in faith, engage in dialogue with them as they call us to greater faithfulness.

The first-person sermon, however, is not the same as a religious play. This is a sermon, not chancel drama. It employs elements of drama, but it must also preach. So it is a story with a point that is driven home. The preacher in the form of the character can interpret, exhort, and invite. We can preach in the character of Peter, making an invitation to faith in Christ even as Peter did repeatedly in the book of Acts.

The first-person sermon opens up a variety of possibilities to the preacher not available in other forms. In other sermon forms, even third-person story-sermons, I have to remain myself while I preach. I speak from my vantage point. In a first-person sermon I can say some things from a different person's vantage point, which can free me to speak in ways I might be unable to as myself. For example, speaking as Pilate, I could make an evangelistic appeal as one who had turned away from Christ, a plea I could not make as my own self. Speaking as Naaman, I can enter into a topic like healing with a vividness that might be harder to generate from my own conceptualization of the emotional issues. The inner dialogue of a character facing a turning point provides an invitation for hearers with similar dialogues to empathize and follow the steps of faith through that character's struggle. The invitation into the soul of another comes across far more powerfully in the first person than in the third person. I provide the bridge into that inner realm rather than leaving it to the hearer to make the leap to where I am pointing.

The first-person format also provides a jolt of freshness in the presentation style. Familiar stories can be heard in new ways. People who shift their minds into cruise control during the sermon have a new opportunity to become engaged. Excitement is generated because the hearers are engaged in the service with parts of themselves usually left dormant. I am not saying that sermons and worship services are usually dull; I am saying that the more of a person that is engaged over time in the act of worship, the more totally consuming worship becomes.

The task in the first-person sermon is preaching, not entertainment. Being cute is spiritually deadly, so one must always keep in mind that the goal is to present the good news more clearly and powerfully for the edification of God's people. One implication of this for me is that I not use the first-person format very often. I use it often enough so that people quickly recognize the form and enter readily and eagerly into the imaginative journey with me. But I don't want to use it so often that it becomes a gimmick or becomes old hat, losing its power. The form must serve the message. If the form becomes the focus, then it's time to reexamine one's preaching as a whole. Done well and done at appropriate intervals, first-person sermons can be vehicles for opening fresh vistas of the gospel to God's people and to us as the preachers.

CHAPTER FOUR

Writing First-Person Sermons

Research

Writing the first-person sermon begins like writing most sermons with a biblical base. You start with your research and exegesis. While an expository sermon will start with a text, however, the first-person sermon starts with a character. Though you may be preaching from a particular text, you may have to draw upon many other passages of Scripture in order to exegete the character thoroughly. For example, in the sermon presented in Part 2 on "Doubting Thomas" in the Easter story, the text is John 20:24-29, but it is impossible to understand Thomas's character without examining the other two texts in the Gospels where Thomas stands apart from the disciples to act and speak. Begin, then, by gathering all the clues given in the Bible about the particular person. Figures like David or Moses may be overwhelming because of the sheer volume of material on them, but they tend to be far better known to us anyway. The lesser-known figures require us to gather every clue we can.

Whether the particular text is the only place where the character appears in the Bible or whether a number of references exist, begin to draw out the specifics so that you can get a sense of the history and character traits of the individual. What clues are we given? Sometimes one word holds much meaning, for example, the identification of Zacchaeus as a tax collector or of Naaman as a leper.

The research then broadens as we look into the significance of those terms and the social contexts the character would dwell in as a result. Even terms that are familiar to the student of the Bible (*tax collector,* for example) need to be pondered. List some of the specific points related to the term, for later these may provide details that will help the character come alive for the hearers.

Also look at the larger historical setting. The story of Naaman cannot be adequately presented unless we know the larger setting of the conflicts between Israel and Syria. Those conflicts give an electricity to the interactions between Naaman and the Israelite king and intensify the prejudices Naaman has to overcome as he seeks help from Elisha. Each character lives in a specific historical moment, which in some stories will have an important bearing on how we understand the dilemmas faced by the character and the grid through which they interpreted the events around them. For characters whose historical setting is important, the preacher will need to be familiar enough with it to make the story a "you were there" experience for the congregation. It will need to be living history, not a dusty forgotten tome. Historical research provides the pool of data that will be drawn upon extensively in the sermon preparation.

Imagination

After completing the research, the preacher must apply imagination. Research is like powdered paint. The powdered paint is essential to the work of art, but it must be mixed with water before it can be used. The research needs to be mixed with imagination. The storyteller-preacher must get into the feelings and experiences of the individual. If the text is recorded in the third person, the preacher needs to step into the skin of the other so as to experience the story in the first person.

Using imagination, put yourself in the character's skin. What does that character see? How are events experienced? What are their significance to the character? What does he or she feel about what is going on? What internal conflicts are triggered by what happens or what is said? Where is the decision point experienced?

How do the feelings change as the situation unfolds? Where is faith challenged or nurtured or exercised? What must be overcome within the character in order for him or her to respond faithfully to God?

Some of the answers to these questions will be provided or pointed toward in the biblical text. But many answers are not given at all. The best way we can answer those questions is to make the human bond between us and the character. Through imagination we exercise our empathy. If the gospel is universal and speaks to us today, we have a common bond with those who first experienced the in-breaking of God into human history. We experience similar hopes, fears, joys, sorrows, loves, hates, angers, and griefs. Our inner heart becomes a lexicon for the feelings of the character. Use that lexicon as one of your orientation points, with the biblical text being the other.

If you are to tell the story fully, your imagination will probably need to be directed to characters other than the one you are assuming in the sermon. To tell the story of Pilate, I must also seek to understand why Jesus says what he says in their dialogue. To tell the story of Naaman, I need to think about the feelings of the Israelite king and Elisha, who reacted so differently to Naaman's request for healing. As the sole dramatist the storytelling preacher needs to be comfortable with all the characters in the story. You cannot play off another actor, so you must use your imagination to make the other characters so vivid that your own response to them will be strikingly clear to the congregation.

Painting the Picture

Having mixed the raw materials of research with imagination, you are ready to start painting the portrait of the character. What is the purpose in telling this story, painting this portrait through dramatic preaching? What are you hoping to achieve? Because this is a sermon and not mere entertainment, a divine work must be envisioned. The purpose may be to bring people to a point of decision, to encourage, to instruct about Christian living, to inspire people to a deeper commitment, to show the way to reconciliation. Whatever the purpose, state it clearly for yourself.

When you have a clear purpose, then you need to decide what format will best achieve that purpose. For some purposes and settings first-person sermons wouldn't work or would be distracting. But if you have decided to do a first-person sermon, what format will you use? Will you do a testimony? Will you do an on-the-scene report? Will you read a letter? Should the character speak directly to the congregation? Or should the character's presentation be made through an imaginary document addressed to a contemporary of the character?

When my dad preached on the centurion at the cross, he preached the story in the third person. He could have also preached it in the first person, speaking directly to the modern congregation as a witness to the events of Jesus' Passion. The sermon could have been reworked as the formal report to his superior officer, which my dad used to give structure to the centurion's reminiscences in the third-person account. Another alternative would be a letter to a colleague, such as the centurion whose child was healed by Jesus, in which he could express the faith issues contained in his affirmation following Jesus' death.

In considering how I as a male could preach a first-person sermon about Mary the mother of Jesus, I was puzzled about how to use a dramatic format with integrity. But the idea of a letter allowed Mary to speak from my lips. Balladeers of centuries past would often sing long songs about characters of a different gender with a prefacing verse about meeting someone who had told the minstrel the tale, so my dramatic mechanism lay in the line of a long tradition. A diary is another format that I could have used as well. It would work, for example, for a character such as Hagar, who had experiences covering a long span of time. Such a format would allow for immediacy, plot development, and character development.

As you begin the process of deciding which format will best serve your purposes and the story, keep in mind the following three considerations: the *range of experiences* to be included, the *message* you wish to convey to the congregation, and the *inner processes* that need to be made explicit.

The format you choose will have implications for the structure of the sermon, so once you are clear about your method of presentation, you can begin constructing the outline. Sketch out the structure of the story on paper. What are the plot movements in the drama, the different acts and scenes? Where are the pivotal points? How should they be ordered?

I once preached a sermon on the story told in John 9 of the man born blind whom Jesus healed. The basic pieces of the story are: his earlier life as a blind beggar, the disciples' theological discussion, the healing by Jesus, the man's interaction with the neighbors, the series of encounters with the Pharisees, his expulsion from the synagogue, and his closing encounter with Jesus. One can tell the story in a linear fashion, or one can begin at the end and then go back to explain how one got there. In this case, I introduced myself to the congregation as the man already healed and spoke to them as if they were his contemporaries. As the man, I was excited about the changes that had taken place in my life and just had to tell someone. I then went back to the beginning of the story to tell of being a blind beggar and the healing encounter with Jesus. In the sermon on Thomas, I followed a linear approach through Thomas's experience as a disciple so that the climax would explode upon the congregation with the same impact that the initial meeting with the risen Christ must have had on Thomas's heart and mind.

Stories flow from the introduction into the development and then to a climax; they then move toward the conclusion, tying up the loose ends or making an application. In the sermon about the blind man, my theme was "telling our faith story," so the climax came when the man gave his testimony before a hostile audience as the Pharisees interrogated him. The initial encounter, when Jesus healed the man, and the closing encounter, in which Jesus revealed that he himself was the messianic "Son of Man," acted as bookends on either side of the climax.

A preacher could choose to organize the material differently to make a different point. The final encounter with Jesus could certainly be made a valid climax; in which case, the discussions with the Pharisees would be seen as leading to the man's developing understanding of and commitment to who Jesus was. The same story can be told in different ways depending on what your purpose is and which elements of the story you wish to emphasize. The introduction needs to present the character and setting at least to such a degree that the listener's interest is aroused. It also serves to present the format to listeners so that they can enter into the experience with understanding. Past and present are linked here. The preacher is inviting the hearer to leave the present and enter into the past, not just as an observer but as someone being empathetically drawn into the story. The bridge into a different time and culture must be clear enough and compelling enough that the congregation can make the transition with ease. If congregants hear a number of well-done first-person sermons, they will be eager to join in the journey, which makes the task of the preacher much easier.

The development usually makes up the bulk of the sermon. The preacher draws heavily at this point upon the details garnered through his or her research and efforts at imaginative empathy. This is where the story must live and the characters breathe. The lines of conflict need to be developed and the dilemmas unfolded so that the challenges and options are seen. The feelings and the plot movement need to be woven together. Keep close tabs on the flow of both the plot and the feelings; if one or the other is lost, the sermon as a whole may lose its way. If the plot takes over, the character is lost; you would do better to preach a third-person sermon. If the feelings take over, the story will bog down; the listeners will have trouble distinguishing your feelings from those of the character. Keep the flow moving. Remember: it's dramatic preaching!

The climax is where God's gospel explodes upon the scene with saving, or in some cases judging, power. The surprising upending of the world's order takes place so that God's order can be established. The decisions made by the characters are revealed for what they are, for good or ill. Structurally, the preacher needs to decide how long to dwell on the climax. Some climaxes are best left bold, blunt, and brilliant. They strike our consciousness like a lightning bolt whose image lasts in our brains beyond the momentary flash. Others can be savored, so that the experience sinks in. The diamond of that moment can be turned to expose its various facets to view. But don't take too long. An artist knows when to stop. More can mean less. Try to sense what presentation of the climax will provide the most clarity and power; then don't undercut the climax by overworking it.

That brings one to the winding down. The moral can be short and sweet, though perhaps with a tartness to it. Aesop's moral at the end of each fable left the hearers with a pithy point to take away. Most of us preachers have a hard time being terse and profound at the same moment. We need more time and words. The winding down could include a plea for response or an exhortation from the character to the congregation. It could consist of the unfolding of the implications of the climax or the events that flowed from that turning point.

This final stage is critical: it is the key moment of interaction between the past and present. You are bringing the hearers back to their lives, back to the context in which they must apply their faith to their challenges. The character can speak directly to them, bridging the centuries by speaking from the wisdom of the experience just related. The purpose of the sermon needs to be recalled, for here that end is either achieved or lost. Here is where a story becomes a sermon. You are not just entertaining from the pulpit; you are delivering God's life-transforming message. Drive the message home. Leave it in the present moment with your contemporaries in the congregation.

The Script

Preachers have their own ways of doing sermons. We may compare our sermon preparation and writing processes with those of other preachers, but we tend to develop our own patterns and habits that work well with our skills and gifts. My style is to outline the sermon and then to preach it in front of the computer. I write down what I preach and preach it again piece by piece as I refine and edit it. Then I print out a complete manuscript. Since it was preached in the preparation stage, I can preach in the pulpit from the manuscript without being bound by that written text. I feel anchored by what I have done, but as I preach I am physically and emotionally free to speak with a full range of bodily and verbal expressions. I should say, though, that I've heard great preaching in just about every format and style imaginable, as has probably every preacher.

When one is doing a first-person sermon, however, a script may be more critical than in a regular sermon. A scripted sermon provides the discipline of attention to the particular words used. Each part is crafted in view of the whole—both the actions related and the words chosen. Writing a script forces the preacher to give extra attention to the selection of words, to the transitions, to the weaving of action and feeling. In a first-person sermon the character provides the unity for the sermon, not the preacher. If not enough discipline is given to maintaining the integrity of the character, the sermon can deteriorate into a message from the preacher. The preacher may be able to give a fine message, but if the format shifts mid-sermon, it will be more of a mess than a message.

A script can be used as the text from which to preach. It can be memorized and delivered without the encumbrance of the preacher's looking at a manuscript. Or, if one prefers to preach from an outline, the script can discipline the thinking done in the study in preparation for that moment when one is in the pulpit with the outline. A greater degree of clarity in the character and in the words used comes from having undertaken the discipline of writing out the script. Use the method that works best for you, but don't shirk the discipline of careful work in crafting a first-person sermon.

CHAPTER FIVE

Preaching First-Person Sermons

Introductions

How does one begin a first-person sermon? How does the preacher move from the flow of a worship service in the present day to a dramatic visitation of a personage from the past? The introduction needs to present a format, perhaps one not seen before, to people in the congregation in such a way that they can rather quickly catch on to what the preacher is doing.

One way is to dive straight into the water of the dramatic sermon, becoming the person as one steps to the pulpit. "My name is Moses!" The abrupt announcement signals that this sermon will differ from the normal Sunday fare, but it also directs the hearers to a familiar biblical setting.

At other times one may want to ease oneself into the water. I can come into the pulpit as myself and introduce the special guest for the morning. I usually like to reserve the declaration of the name for the character's presentation, so I may say some words about the time of the church year and point out that an eyewitness can help us gain a better understanding of the events we commemorate. Following this brief introduction I take a step back, pause, then step up to the pulpit in the character of the biblical or historical figure.

Simple acts can carry dramatic weight, whereas overacting will come across as too cute. The transition serves the presentation of the message, so it must be kept as spare and pertinent as possible. If the preacher presents first-person sermons often enough, even a few times a year, a stylized form of introduction will quickly signal to the congregation that another dramatic sermon is coming. They will recognize the form immediately and usually respond with expectancy and increased interest. Stick with an introductory formula that feels comfortable to you, adjusting it in special cases.

One such case is when the biblical character is of a gender different from the preacher's. As I noted above, when I preached as Mary, I had to figure out a way to speak authentically in her voice. The format of a letter written by Mary to Elizabeth allowed me to do that. I invited the congregation to join me in an exercise of the imagination in which archeologists had found such a letter. The voice could then be feminine even through this male preacher. A report or journal from a character could also serve as an effective transgender dramatic vehicle. Again, simplicity is vital in keeping the focus on the message. The idea of the dramatic vehicle must be clear and must be communicated quickly. Another case is when the biblical character is not an exemplar of faith. When I preached as Pontius Pilate, I used the introduction both to set him apart from the believing community and also to give him the opportunity to speak.

The introduction works well if it takes care of the necessary business of getting the hearers on board with the dramatic process. If you start the first-person sermon with everyone clear about who you are and where you are going, then they are likely to stay with you the rest of the way, assuming that you maintain the format and keep their interest!

Dramatic Style

A story must be experienced, not analyzed. So the preacher has to re-create the initial experience through the power of storytelling, probably with no sets or costumes. Your tools are word, voice, body, and imagination. We preachers tend to do best with the words, but dramatic preaching often involves a fuller range of voice and body language than a conventional homily.

Ranges of emotion cannot just be described; they must be fully expressed. When I preached as Pontius Pilate, I used my voice to project the image of the bored, cynical administrator who was awakened too early at the initial encounter with Jesus. Then as the trial of Jesus wore on and Pilate was confronted with a profound moral choice by the one he thought he was trying, Pilate's voice moved to confusion and even desperate rage. I yelled out Pilate's attempt to maintain control of his judgeship, though yelling is not something I do in my regular sermons. The emotion drives the voice. The preacher must loosen any restraints on his or her voice so that the full impact of the character's emotional state can be directly experienced.

The children's program *Sesame Street* sometimes shows faces and asks children to identify the emotions and feelings of the person. They respond, "Angry, sad, surprised, afraid, happy, goofy" or whatever word labels the emotion expressed in the face. Let your voice and your body give such a clear audio-picture to the congregation members that they can instantly identify what is going on.

One's body is a dramatic tool as well, so use it, even more than you might in your standard sermon. When the character is afraid, hunch your shoulders and cower even as you speak. When she is angry, swell up and rise on your feet like a roiling thunderhead. When he is hurt, draw in protectively and perhaps close your eyes. When she is confused, turn from side to side.

As one person you can easily locate a second character in the drama by speaking to a certain space as the second person. In dialogues with God one can look up and gesture upward. When I preached as Pilate, Jesus was located at the altar to the left of the pulpit, and the crowd was in the pews. Which way I faced and where I directed my voice made their presence dramatically vivid.

When one preaches as a biblical or historical character, the challenge is to make clear the movement of grace and faith so that the congregation can understand. These are interior dynamics, which are usually very much rooted in the exterior flow of history, events, and relationships. But the interior dynamics are what turn the encounters into salvation history. Two people can be present at the same time; one responds to the presence of grace, while the other doesn't. The classic case is the two thieves crucified on either side of Jesus. One cursed, while the other asked to be welcomed into Christ's kingdom. The dramatic preacher needs to make the interior spiritual and ethical journey of a character visible to the congregation. How can the hearer come empathetically to understand the inner dilemmas and decisions of that ancient person? What brings that person to the encounter with God? How does the character wrestle through a decision in response to God? How does the character move from one inner state to another? Your voice and body unlock the imagination of the congregation for this inner journey, so fully use these keys in your preaching.

Script

If you have not memorized your sermon but are using a manuscript, you can prepare your manuscript to be more easily used in a dramatic presentation. Some of these suggestions may help to free you from the text so that you can give fuller dramatic expression during the preaching.

If the manuscript is laid out in paragraphs (as are the sermons printed in this book), it is difficult for the eye to quickly spot the right place. Breaking the text out into separate sentences in a semi–outline style allows the eye to search more quickly for the place. Longer sentences can also be indented on the second and subsequent lines so that the beginning point of each sentence stands out visually.

The following paragraph is from the sermon on Zacchaeus printed in this book, but here it is laid out for use in the pulpit:

"As head tax collector I had a lot of other guys working for
    me doing the same thing.
And of course, I raked off a certain percentage of
    their profits, too.
With all this money coming in, I was one of the
    wealthiest guys in town.
I mean, I was loaded!

> I had a big, beautiful house, wore fancy clothes and
> expensive rings, and ate at the finest restaurants.
> You would think I had it made, wouldn't you?"

Extra double spaces help break up the text further into thematic blocks. Quotations from Scripture or from other characters can be set off in blocks.

Multicolored highlighting markers can be used as quick reference pointers in the text. One color can be used to mark the major theme of a paragraph. Another can mark Scripture to be quoted. Yet another color can set off "stage directions" to yourself if you wish to insert them.

In some cases I have preached from multiple locations. I positioned portions of my manuscript in those places around the chancel, sometimes on a music stand, so that I could move freely from one spot to the other. The text was there waiting for me with all the visual cues so I could maintain the pace of the presentation.

These ideas and others you may have developed can be incorporated into all sermons using manuscripts. However, the more dramatic one hopes to be, the more cumbersome a manuscript becomes. Given that most pastors have to have a fresh sermon every seven days and that most of us have not developed good memorizing skills, we may require a manuscript, restricting though it often is. So every aid we can employ to get a boost from manuscript to dramatic presentation is worth using.

Closing

Closing the sermon involves not only a transition to the next part of the worship service but a transition of time and personage. The pastor has to come back. This shift can be made in a number of ways. The preacher will need to decide how best to make the shift on the basis of where the sermon leaves the hearers and what comes next in the service.

Some formats will contain their own close. The letter from Mary to Elizabeth ends as a letter would. When I had finished reading it, I was obviously back in my own self and voice. First-person sermons structured as a report or as journal entries can be written to contain the close in themselves. A simple change in the tone of voice and a look at the congregation can signal your return to the present.

On the other hand, the character may actually be used to move the service into the next element. If the sermon is evangelistic, the character can make the appeal for decision. I added an invitation for people to commit themselves to Christ at the end of Pontius Pilate's message and of Zacchaeus's. Naaman invited people to come for healing. Then I had to pick up my pastoral role as the invitation proceeded. That could be done by moving from the pulpit, saying, "You have heard the testimony of _____ about Jesus, so what will you do?" The physical move from the place where you spoke in character gives a visual break to go along with the verbal shift. Coming down from the pulpit also brings you as pastor to the place to meet those who would respond to the invitation.

The preacher can handle the transition by making a brief physical shift, stepping out of the pulpit and then back up again to pray, moving to the side of the pulpit to announce a hymn, or even sitting down and then standing up in a pastoral role. If you decide to preach a number of first-person sermons, experiment with the transition movements that feel most natural to you. If a small vestment or costume change was made when one assumed the role of the biblical character, reversing the change makes a clear return to the pastoral role. When I set aside the stole to become Pontius Pilate, upon concluding the sermon I put the stole back on again.

Sometimes the transition works best if handled by others leading in worship. Another person may pray or introduce a hymn. Having another person pray can be risky, however. The prayer may erode the power of the message if it is too wordy, if it picks up a secondary theme, or if it tries to play along with the dramatic presentation too much. Whoever is to pray should be informed about the sermon, how it will end, and perhaps coached on how to lead in a transitional prayer appropriate to the message. To avoid involving another person verbally in the transition, the preacher could simply sit down following the end of the message, and the organist could start playing a hymn.

There is no curtain call for a dramatic sermon. The preacher should not be the center of attention. Christ is the one who should be lifted up; if the dramatic form has gotten in the way of Christ and the gospel story, then the preacher has failed in the divinely commissioned task. The closing should serve to get the preacher's dramatic character off the stage so that the work of God in the hearts of the worshippers can continue. The work of the preacher is intimately woven in with God's work, but our attitudes as preachers should always reflect that of John the Baptist: that Christ should increase, and we should decrease.

There's an old saying: "the proof of the pudding is in the eating." Likewise, the proof of a sermon is in the preaching. The ten following first-person sermons were all preached at least once; some have been preached several times in different settings. The sermons are reprinted here both for your own edification and also as examples of the first-person form. They can be read solely as devotional or inspirational texts, but I have also intended a larger purpose. For the preachers who wish to polish their own skills through interaction with another preacher, I have appended "preacher-to-preacher notes." These notes provide a behind-the-scenes look into my preparation and thought processes as I wrote and preached each sermon. The notes are not a defense of my choices but are a transparent sampling of the kind of issues and decisions a preacher of first-person sermons might face. I hope the sermons that follow will be not only instructive for homiletical purposes but will also be a blessing to each reader.

PART TWO

Sermons in the First Person

Testimony of Thomas

TEXT: JOHN 20:19-29

When it was evening on that day, the first day of the week, and the doors of the house where the disciples had met were locked for fear of the Jews, Jesus came and stood among them and said, "Peace be with you." After he said this, he showed them his hands and his side. Then the disciples rejoiced when they saw the Lord. Jesus said to them again, "Peace be with you. As the Father has sent me, so I send you." When he had said this, he breathed on them and said to them, "Receive the Holy Spirit. If you forgive the sins of any, they are forgiven them; if you retain the sins of any, they are retained."

But Thomas (who was called the Twin), one of the twelve, was not with them when Jesus came. So the other disciples told him, "We have seen the Lord." But he said to them, "Unless I see the mark of the nails in his hands, and put my finger in the mark of the nails and my hand in his side, I will not believe."

A week later his disciples were again in the house, and Thomas was with them. Although the doors were shut, Jesus came and stood among them and said, "Peace be with you." Then he said to Thomas, "Put your finger here and see my hands. Reach out your hand and put it in my side. Do not doubt but believe." Thomas answered him, "My Lord and my God!" Jesus said to him, "Have you believed because you have seen me? Blessed are those who have not seen and yet have come to believe."

I could preach a sermon this morning about the resurrection of Jesus, but instead I've asked an actual eyewitness to share his story with us.

Good morning! My name is Thomas, "Doubting Thomas" to some, but I think a lot of people misunderstand my doubt. Some people think of it as a rational or intellectual doubt, but that's hardly my nature. I'm a rather impulsive fellow, always doing things in the heat of the moment, thinking before I act. What I lack in brains I make up for in enthusiasm. But that's what got me into trouble. I was operating by my feelings, my enthusiasm, my impulses, but I didn't really understand what Jesus was all about. So let me tell you what happened.

I was one of the early followers of Jesus. He called me to leave my fishing trade and follow him, just as he had a number of other fishermen. This man Jesus gave my life a real sense of direction, a purpose that excited and challenged me.

He came preaching about the kingdom of God. He said that God was coming to welcome the common folks, folks like me, to be his people. God wasn't distant from us but was very near to us. God heard our secret prayers and invited us to call him our Father. He also gave us the challenge to follow, to break out of the old patterns and learn to live following his example. He promised us life in all its fullness if we would trust God in a radical way for everything.

But it wasn't the words so much as the man, who he was. His words were spoken with authority, like he knew the truth and had no doubt about it. He wasn't cocky though, or arrogant, like he had to prove who he was. He knew who he was and was confident in the truth God had given him. Time after time, miracle after miracle, teaching after teaching, we saw the power and gentleness, the love and authority of this man. It wasn't so much what he said but who he was that drew me to him.

So for three years I followed Jesus everywhere he went. He chose me to be one of his inner circle, one of the twelve apostles. I don't know why he chose me. Maybe he saw my zeal, and he thought he could channel all that enthusiasm into a positive direction. But during those three years I came to believe passionately in Jesus. I didn't understand everything he said or did, but his influence was stretching me beyond everything I'd ever experienced before. He made me feel so close to God, and he made me do things I had never dreamed I could do.

My hopes were high. I was on fire, zealous for the kingdom of God. My life had never seemed so purposeful, and I thought God was just wonderful.

But then it all began to come apart for me, and for all us disciples. And Jesus was causing it to happen.

He had gone up to Jerusalem for the Feast of Tabernacles, a big religious holiday for us Jews. While there he got into serious trouble with the powers that be over some of his teachings. People got so stirred up that they tried to arrest him and lynch him, but somehow we managed to slip away and got safely back to Galilee. So we knew Jerusalem was going to be trouble for Jesus.

For a few months after that things went okay, but then Lazarus, a close friend of Jesus, became seriously ill. Lazarus lived just outside Jerusalem in the village of Bethany. So when Jesus found out about Lazarus's being sick, he said, "Let's go back to Judea again." And, O wow, all the disciples got upset! "Are you crazy, Jesus? Last time you were there you almost got killed, and you want to go back again!" They all tried to talk him out of it, but when Jesus knew what he wanted to do, he always did it.

I knew we couldn't stop him from going back to the Jerusalem area, so I chimed in, "Let's all go along, so that we may die with him!" Sounds noble and grand, doesn't it? So full of enthusiasm, so dedicated. So shallow. I understood so little about myself or about Jesus. As I look back, knowing that I fled into the darkness that night he was arrested, those words sure sound empty. Somehow I didn't really believe he would die. If God was with him, surely nothing too bad would happen. So I could be noble and courageous. I could be full of faith, because the tough times were still in the distance.

Well, we went to Jerusalem, and it was the time of the Feast of the Passover, our biggest and most important religious festival. Hundreds of thousands of people come into the city then. Jesus had just raised Lazarus from the dead, which made his friends more excited and his enemies more furious. Everybody was tense. You could feel the coming confrontation in the air.

Did Jesus try to keep things cool and avoid trouble like he had in the past? Exactly the opposite. He came into the city on a young donkey colt, an act that was a statement to the people: "I am your Messiah!" That was how the prophet Zechariah had said the Messiah would come, riding on a donkey colt, and here was Jesus doing it! The crowds burst into a grand parade, following Jesus down the road from the Mount of Olives into the city.

And he went straight into the temple, turned over the tables where they were doing business, chased out all the hucksters and money changers, and began to teach right there under the noses of the religious leaders. Jesus was deliberately bringing the conflict to a head.

I began to get scared. My zeal began to shrink away and was replaced by confusion. What was Jesus doing? Didn't he realize how foolish he was acting? Didn't he know the power of the temple authorities? Didn't he know the power of the Roman army that would crush any public disturbance without mercy? He had a good thing going with his friends, but we weren't ready to take on all the might of the religious and political establishment.

Thursday night we gathered together for the Passover meal, and Jesus started acting very strange. He washed our feet, something only a slave should do, and he said we were to do the same for one another. He said the bread was his body to be broken for us, and he said the wine was his blood poured out for the forgiveness of sins. I didn't understand. I was confused. Was he saying good-bye to us?

Jesus said, "I am going to prepare a place for you. And I will come back and take you to myself, so that you will be where I am. You know how to get to the place where I am going." But I didn't know. I hadn't the faintest idea what was going on. Did he have some sort of secret hideout where he could stay till everything blew over? So I said, "Lord, we do not know where you are going. How can we know the way to get there?"

He looked at me with eyes longing for me to understand and said, "I am the way, the truth, and the life; no one goes to the Father except by me." But that didn't make any sense to me. Something bad was happening. Jesus was leaving us, and three years of my life were coming to a confusing, frustrating end.

The next few hours so much happened that I was in a state of shock. We left the upper room where we were staying and went out to the garden of Gethsemane. Jesus started to pray, but I fell asleep.

Suddenly, angry voices woke me up. A crowd of soldiers and men with clubs and torches were almost upon us. Then Judas—my friend, Judas—stepped out of the mob, came up to Jesus, and kissed him. Immediately the soldiers seized him, and we all fled. I never looked back. I ran and ran and ran and finally found a place to hide until morning.

The next day I slipped in with the crowds coming into the city, and there on the town dump I saw three crosses. Jesus was hanging on the middle one. I felt sick to my stomach as I looked at the pain on his face, as I saw his chest heaving, straining for breath. Through the heat of the day, through the terrible thunderstorm that came, I stood there and watched him die. Oh, what an awful way to die. Why, God, why did you let this happen?

I died up there, too. All that had seemed to bloom in my life withered. Have you ever had your hopes crushed, your dreams shattered? That's how I felt. Life is a raw deal. The only decent person I had ever met died a horrible death in front of me, and it was God's fault. It's just not fair! I'd trusted in him so much, and I got burned.

For three or four days I wandered around the city in a daze. All the bitterness and anger soon seeped away, and I was left with a huge emptiness inside that hurt. Jesus was gone. No more could I hear his voice. No more could I see his love change people's lives. No more could I listen to his words of comfort and power. Jesus was gone, and with him my hope that God could make something good out of this mess called life. I sank into a deep depression. For hours I would simply sit at a table in one of the inns and just ache inside.

Somehow, after a few days, one of the disciples found me, and he shared some incredible news. He said Jesus was alive! He said Jesus had appeared to them in the upper room. He had spoken to them and eaten with them.

Have you ever had someone tell you things are going well, and you know they aren't? Someone is dying, and you say, "Get well soon," or "You're looking better every day." It's a lie, and you know it. That's what this story seemed to me. Those other disciples were just denying what had happened. Hadn't they seen his final agony, too? I could still see the nails that tore his flesh. I could still see that Roman guard slam the spear into his side. "If I don't see the scars of the nails in his hands, and put my finger on those scars, and my hand in his side, I will not believe!" There, I'd told 'em.

But they persuaded me to come along and join them. So I did. I had to begin to put my life back together somehow.

We were all together in the upper room. The doors were locked because we were afraid the Roman soldiers might arrest us for being followers of Jesus. Suddenly, Jesus appeared right in the middle of the room and said, "Peace be with you."

My heart jumped up into my throat. He was there, solid as ever. No phantom, no dream, no doubt about it. But he wasn't normal, like you or me. Instead he had a certain glory to his appearance. He was radiant, full of energy, full of life. No more trace of weariness about him; instead there was a sense of total triumph.

He reached out his hands toward me and said: "Thomas, put your finger here, and look at my hands; then stretch out your hand and put it in my side. Stop your doubting, and believe!" Oh, the wounds were there. The torn flesh where the nails had been. That awful slash in his side. The marks of his torture were still fresh, but they had no power over him. He seemed fully human, but more. There he was bodily before me, the same Jesus who had been crucified a few short days before. But now death had no part of him at all.

And I began to understand. I thought I had known who Jesus was, but I had such little ideas. My idea of God had been too small. This man I thought I knew was no mere human—he was God in human flesh. He was the Lord of life! Love and power and joy and peace poured out from his presence. What I had only caught glimpses of before was now completely open in Jesus. Now I knew who he really was.

It began to dawn upon me that Jesus had won the victory over death by plunging straight into the middle of human suffering and sorrow, dying himself on that cross. There the power of his love broke the stranglehold of death, and he was beyond it all forever. He was the victor over all that tastes of death and corruption.

I was humbled before him. My words of doubt fled away. My despair was gone. My bitterness turned to joy. I fell down on my knees and said, "My Lord and my God!" What else can one say in the presence of the Lord of life? "My Lord and my God! Whatever I am, Jesus, I am yours!"

Why am I telling you my story? Jesus told me, "Do you believe because you see me? How happy are those who believe without seeing me!" I was an eyewitness to the risen Christ not because I had great faith but because God in divine grace came to me when I was confused and broken and full of despair. I saw God win the victory over death. I know without a doubt that there is more to this life than meets the eye, for I have seen Christ overcome the heart of darkness by the light of his love.

Jesus Christ is risen from the dead! And even today his resurrection power is changing people's lives, just as he changed mine. Jesus can touch your life wherever you are and replace your confusion with understanding, your despair with hope, your doubt with faith. Jesus Christ is risen! If you open your eyes of faith and see him, you too will exclaim, "My Lord and my God!"

Preacher-to-Preacher Notes

Easter Sunday is always a challenge because we have this one theme, albeit a powerful and central one for our faith, to preach upon every year. The church usually has its highest attendance for the year. Telling the story through the immediacy of an eyewitness experience allows the preacher to present the resurrection message without getting bogged down in too much theologizing. For a crowd with a high percentage of nonregular attenders, the story will probably penetrate to the soul better than something abstract.

Thomas has an emotional life with which many of us can identify. We know hope and disappointment. We know confusion following the collapse of mental categories that had once held our understanding so neatly. Those who journey with Thomas can find themselves coming to the moment of revelation where they too see the risen Christ. This sermon sets up an invitation to faith for those who have never seen but are ready to believe.

I came to the idea of this sermon when I decided to study Thomas as a person rather than just preach on the postresurrection encounter recorded in John. In the three times that Thomas is recorded speaking we find a character that is more complex than the mere caricature of "Doubting Thomas." He is seen as a person of passion, willing to risk following Jesus into danger when everyone else is trying to be the voice of reason. He is also a person who relates to what is directly experienced, sometimes not getting the deeper meaning of words or events. To preach a first-person sermon, one must gather all the evidence about a person's character and then feel those various pieces of the portrait. In Thomas's case I found the result a more interesting and appealing person with whom I could readily identify.

You may have noted the use of the word *and* in this sermon. Some grammarians frown upon using *And* at the beginning of a sentence, but good storytelling doesn't necessarily follow the strictest grammatical rules. *And* can convey a sense of urgency or a sense of events or thoughts tumbling one after another. Mark's Gospel is full of the word *and*, though many of the English translations delete some of the *kai*s that appear in the Greek. Mark's Gospel is the one closest to the oral story, of Peter and perhaps of Mark himself. Mark rushes through the stories propelled by the urgency of the mission of Jesus. At times our first-person stories pick up momentum, and the use of the word *and* can be a verbal and grammatical engine for maintaining or increasing the momentum.

And can also be used to string along a list of words to accent them equally and fully for the listener. One could write the sentence thus: "Love, power, joy, and peace poured out from his presence." But preached that way, the list has less power. If the preacher wants to emphasize the list or linger on each word, *and* is the better connector: "Love and power and joy and peace poured out from his presence!"

Pontius Pilate:
Testimony of an Unbeliever

TEXT: JOHN 18:33-38; 19:7-11, 16

Then Pilate entered the headquarters again, summoned Jesus, and asked him, "Are you the King of the Jews?" Jesus answered, "Do you ask this on your own, or did others tell you about me?" Pilate replied, "I am not a Jew, am I? Your own nation and the chief priests have handed you over to me. What have you done?" Jesus answered, "My kingdom is not from this world. If my kingdom were from this world, my followers would be fighting to keep me from being handed over to the Jews. But as it is, my kingdom is not from here." Pilate asked him, "So you are a king?" Jesus answered, "You say that I am a king. For this I was born, and for this I came into the world, to testify to the truth. Everyone who belongs to the truth listens to my voice." Pilate asked him, "What is truth?" . . .

. . . The Jews answered him, "We have a law, and according to that law he ought to die because he has claimed to be the Son of God."

Now when Pilate heard this, he was more afraid than ever. He entered his headquarters again and asked Jesus, "Where are you from?" But Jesus gave him no answer. Pilate therefore said to him, "Do you refuse to speak to me? Do you not know that I have power to release you, and power to crucify you?" Jesus answered him, "You would have no power over me unless it had been given

you from above; therefore the one who handed me over
to you is guilty of a greater sin."
    Then he handed him over to them to be crucified.

I'm not in the habit of letting an unbeliever preach from the
pulpit, but I'm going to make an exception today; for this man,
though he is an unbeliever, has a message we need to hear. So
please, extend a measure of courtesy and decency to our guest this
morning and hear him out. May I introduce to you Pontius Pilate.

Good morning. You probably know me just as the man who
sentenced your Lord Jesus to die. But I have a place in history
beyond that. I was Roman procurator, or governor, of Judea under
the Roman Empire for ten years during the reign of Emperor
Tiberius.

I had a number of run-ins with the Jews, whom I considered a
contentious, uncivilized lot who were prone to riot and revolt and
who had all sorts of stupid religious scruples. More than once I used
my crack Roman troops to put down disturbances with force. I can't
say I was loved—in fact I was despised by most of the Jews, even
those who were loyal to Rome. After ten rocky years I was called
back to Rome because of a particularly brutal end I made to a
Samaritan uprising.

As you can imagine, I haven't gotten very favorable press in
either Jewish or Christian circles, but I'm not here today to defend
myself. I'm here to tell you about my encounter with Jesus in the
hope that you won't make the same mistakes I made. It's too late
for me now, but not for you.

I met Jesus on the Friday before the big Jewish religious feast of
Passover. It was early in the morning—the sun was just coming up.
I hadn't eaten breakfast yet, and I was not too kindly disposed to
have a case brought before me so early. They brought a man named
Jesus of Nazareth for me to try. They said he was "perverting their
nation and claiming he was a king."

Well, it seemed to be a pretty minor case—I'd never even heard
of the guy. I wasn't particularly interested in dealing with it at six
o'clock in the morning! So I said, "You yourselves take him and

try him according to your own law." But the Jewish leaders replied, "We are not allowed to put anyone to death."

So they wanted this Jesus killed, and killed soon. It was a capital case, and all death sentences had to pass through me for ratification.

So I went back into the praetorium, my Jerusalem headquarters and residence, to question the prisoner who had been handed over to my own guards. Let me tell you that no prisoner looks very imposing when chained between highly skilled Roman soldiers. I approached Jesus with something of a cynical smirk. I'd met enough rabble-rousers who thought they could throw us Romans out of their country—but they'd all been easily squashed. So I asked him, "Are you the king of the Jews?" His answer took me back a bit. His eyes looked into mine in a probing way: "Does this question come from you, or have others told you about me?" I felt he was shifting the focus from himself to me—he wanted to put me on the spot. What did I really think? Was I going to listen to him or not?

I shrugged off his question. "Do you think I am a Jew? It was your own people and the chief priests who handed you over to me. What have you done?" Jesus said: "My kingdom does not belong to this world; if my kingdom belonged to this world, my followers would fight to keep me from being handed over to the authorities. No, my kingdom does not belong here!"

Then I said, "So you are a king?" Perhaps in some sort of harmless, spiritualized, fantasy realm, I thought. But Jesus was serious. His eyes held mine, and he refused to let me shrug him off. "You say that I am a king. I was born and came into the world for this one purpose, to speak about the truth. Whoever belongs to the truth listens to me." That was a powerful, heady statement, and I didn't feel I wanted to probe further. This man was unsettling to me, and I wasn't sure I wanted to pursue the course he was taking me on.

So I closed our interview saying, "What is truth?" I've seen it all; everyone is out for something. They all have their price; they all sell out or else are beaten down. What is truth in a world that works by power and might? So I waved for the guards to haul him away.

But let me tell you, I was starting to churn inside. Jesus was reaching out to me. He wanted me to listen, but not to a defense from a man on trial. Not once did he try to save his life or refute the charges against him. He wanted me to listen to the truth, to hear his message. I could feel him commanding my attention, even my allegiance. It was there in his eyes, in his stance. Who's in charge here anyway? I'm the governor! I'm the judge!

Only now, looking back, can I see that everyone else involved in the death of Jesus had heard him speak. They knew what he was about and were therefore responsible for their rejection of his word. But I knew nothing, and so Jesus was giving me a chance.

This one who was divine truth in human flesh was standing before me, trying to get my attention.

And I shut him off with a question: "What is truth?" He could answer it: "I am the truth, the way, the life." But my question wasn't sincere. It was a cynical way of saying that there are no answers. So often we use questions not to learn or understand but to shut off discussion. I now see that this is dishonest and cynical, and it cuts us off from God. God wants to answer our real, heartfelt questions, the honest inquiries of searching minds. God wants those who seek to find, but I knew Jesus was seeking me, so I played a hide-and-seek game using my verbal smoke screen: "What is truth?"

I went back to the courtyard where the crowd was gathered. I tried to kill two birds with one stone. "I find this man innocent," I said. He seemed harmless enough. But I could say he was guilty and then turn him loose as part of my custom to free one prisoner at Passover. It was a custom I had developed to keep the peace by making a magnanimous gesture of our Roman mercy once a year. I could placate the crowd by giving them the guilty verdict, but then still have the innocent man freed. So I asked the crowd if they wanted Jesus set free under my governor's pardon. He would still bear the shame of the conviction if not the penalty of death. It seemed a reasonable compromise.

But my ploy didn't work; it backfired. The crowd began to scream for the release of Barabbas instead. I couldn't believe it!

Barabbas was a real hard-core criminal—a thief, a murderer. Why would they want Barabbas set free instead of this harmless guy with his seeming delusions of grandeur?

So I decided to have my soldiers work Jesus over a bit. A little beating and mockery might satisfy their blood lust. My soldiers put a crown of thorns and a purple robe on him. They beat him up pretty good and jeered at him. I brought him out with me onto the platform overlooking the crowd and yelled: "Look at the man!"—he had been bruised, battered, and ridiculed. But instead of being satisfied, the crowd went crazy. They began to yell: "Crucify him, crucify him, crucify him!"

I tried to argue that I saw no reason to condemn him, but then someone yelled, "We have a law that says he ought to die because he claimed to be the Son of God." The Son of God? Who is this man?

Just then my wife had a note passed to me. She had written: "Have nothing to do with this righteous man, for I have suffered much over him today in a dream." I was deeply troubled; something strange, something eerie, was going on. Who was this man? He seemed so innocent, so harmless, yet there was a power in his presence that bothered me. This was no ordinary offender, no ordinary trial.

So I went back inside to speak once more with Jesus: "Where are you from?" He wouldn't answer. I think he knew I didn't really want to know. I wanted to be comfortable, not to be bothered with this troublesome, perplexing man. His eyes seemed to be saying, "You've figured it out, Pilate, but you don't want to admit it, do you?"

His silence infuriated me: "You won't speak to me? Remember, I have the authority to set you free and also to have you crucified." But he wouldn't bow to my bullying: "You have authority over me only because it was given to you by God. So the man who handed me over to you is guilty of a worse sin."

I knew I was trapped now. Jesus was innocent before the law—I could clearly see that—but he wasn't going to play any legal games to save his own skin. He wasn't even going to defend himself. It was up to me. I was the judge; the decision was mine.

So I passed sentence. After one final attempt to pacify his accusers—an attempt that completely failed—I called for a bowl of water and washed my hands before them all. "I am innocent of this man's blood." But it was an empty gesture, for I was the one who turned him over to my own soldiers to be executed. And my men very efficiently carried out their duties.

Let me tell you, I failed. At the most critical decision point of my life, I failed miserably. I missed my moment with God.

The truth of God in human flesh was standing in front of me. Jesus was trying to reach me, and I got the idea of who he was. It wasn't crystal clear to me, but it was there.

And I deliberately closed the door. I slammed shut the door of my heart in the face of God. I closed myself off with cynicism because I didn't really want to know the truth. I closed myself off with fear because the cost to stand with Jesus was higher than I wanted to pay. I closed myself off by shrugging off my responsibility.

I pretended to myself that the choice wasn't mine. I blamed someone else—the crowd, the religious leaders, even Jesus' stubbornness in not defending himself. But the choice was mine. I had no excuse. It was I who sentenced him to die—and in doing so I passed sentence upon my own self. I sentenced myself to a life without God, a life of tragic independence from Christ, a life, ultimately, of hell.

And you are no different from me. Jesus is standing before you.

He is the truth, the living truth of God. He is the sovereign Lord claiming your loyalty and allegiance. He is reaching out to you, trying to get you to follow him and know his life and joy. What are you going to do with him? What is your sentence?

Will you sentence Jesus to die? You do that every time you say no to Jesus. You provide one more reason for him to be nailed to the cross. You pass the death sentence through cynicism when you won't commit yourself to anything but instead hide behind phony questions and criticisms. You pass the death sentence through fear by giving in to the pressure to conform to the world and go along with the crowd. You pass the death sentence by shrugging off your responsibility, saying you don't have to decide, not today.

But today is the day. Now is the time we choose for Christ. And if you choose *for* Christ, you choose life for yourself, abundant life, eternal life.

Don't be foolish as I was and send him away. Rather come, give your life to him, commit yourself to follow him to the cross, and die to your old self. Join him as he leads you into the new life, the resurrection life, the Easter life, that he longs to give you. The choice is yours—the time is now. What will you do?

Preacher-to-Preacher Notes

I came up with the idea for this sermon as I was studying the Passion story in John's Gospel. I was taken by the conversations recorded between Jesus and Pilate. As I reflected upon them, it seemed that Jesus was bringing Pilate to a decision point. It was an evangelistic moment. To turn the perspective of the event upside down for us Christians and view Jesus through the eyes of Pilate would provide both a fresh view of a familiar story and open up the dynamics of spiritual decision.

Throughout the sermon I tried to mirror Pilate's emotional progress. I began with a cynical, arrogant demeanor. Then, as Pilate began to puzzle about Jesus, I tried to convey some of his internal conflict, his questions amid the intensity of trying to assert his control. I almost screamed out in rage, "I'm the governor! I'm the judge!" Toward the end of the message the tone was that of a broken man resigned to having made a terrible decision, but with a light of hope for some redemption if his plea could help save others.

After introducing Pontius Pilate, I performed a simple act that separated me as the preacher from the character I was assuming. I stepped back from the pulpit, took off my stole, laid it over a chair, and then stepped back to the pulpit. The ministerial robe was transformed into a judicial robe without my saying a word. A number in the congregation told me later how effective that simple act was. It enabled them to make the role shift with me smoothly and quickly. Drama doesn't need elaborate sets to transport the viewer-listener into another time and place. Evocative sets or actions in their stark simplicity can do an even more powerful job because they make the congregation's imagination an ally of the preacher.

While working on the text of this book, I stumbled across a delightful work by James R. Mills: *The Gospel According to*

Pontius Pilate. Mills has produced an imaginative memoir and history of the events surrounding Jesus as written by Pilate in his retirement. The purpose of Pilate's memoir was to explain who these Christians were during the years of Nero's persecution. In Mills's book Pilate remains within the confines of his historical personage, whereas in this sermon Pilate is envisioned as coming back from the dead to appeal directly to hearers centuries later. My sermon is in line with the rich man's request, in the parable about the rich man and Lazarus, to send someone from the dead to urge his brothers to repent. The request denied by Abraham is granted in a fashion by the first-person preacher.

A Letter from Mary

In that region there were shepherds living in the fields, keeping watch over their flock by night. Then an angel of the Lord stood before them, and the glory of the Lord shone around them, and they were terrified. But the angel said to them, "Do not be afraid; for see—I am bringing you good news of great joy for all the people: to you is born this day in the city of David a Savior, who is the Messiah, the Lord. This will be a sign for you: you will find a child wrapped in bands of cloth and lying in a manger." And suddenly there was with the angel a multitude of the heavenly host, praising God and saying, "Glory to God in the highest heaven, and on earth peace among those whom he favors!"

When the angels had left them and gone into heaven, the shepherds said to one another, "Let us go now to Bethlehem and see this thing that has taken place, which the Lord has made known to us." So they went with haste and found Mary and Joseph, and the child lying in the manger. When they saw this, they made known what had been told them about this child; and all who heard it were amazed at what the shepherds told them. But Mary treasured all these words and pondered them in her heart. The shepherds returned, glorifying and praising God for all they had heard and seen, as it had been told them.

Use your imagination with me if you will. Imagine that through the wonders of modern archeology we have discovered a letter sent by Mary the mother of Jesus to her cousin Elizabeth. So let's receive this treasure of a primary source about the events we celebrate that took place so long ago.

Dear Elizabeth,

It's a boy! That should come as no surprise to you after what we've both experienced. But though the angel told me I would bear a son, nothing prepared me for the events of the past few weeks.

After my visit to you before your dear little John was born, I went back to Nazareth. Joseph and I were married—oh, how the tongues wagged! I was beginning to show by then, and of course, nobody would have believed I was still a virgin! The angel told me I had found favor with God, but I certainly didn't find favor with the women of Nazareth. The shame my neighbors heaped upon me drained away much of the awe and joy I received from the angel's visit and my time with you. How I longed for your strength, support, and understanding! At least I have had Joseph to share the stigma with me. He has been such a blessing ever since the angel appeared to him and let him in on this secret miracle.

As you know, the Romans made us all go to our patriarchal homes for a tax census. Joseph, being a descendant of David, had to go to Bethlehem, so we set off with our donkey, which I rode. Joseph carried the knapsack with our food and bedding. It took five days to reach Bethlehem, but they all became a blur to me. The child was low, so near the time of delivery, and each step of the donkey jarred my heavy body.

When we arrived at Bethlehem, we found everything in confusion. The Roman bureaucrat who organized this census must have hit on the idea while drunk at a party. At least he never gave any consideration for the tremendous problems and inconveniences it imposed on people. People were everywhere—I never knew there were so many people of David's house. Families were camped all along the roads leading into town. The inn was filled to overflowing. Though we had camped the other nights of our journey, we couldn't on this night. The baby was coming, and we had to find shelter from the chill of the night air.

My labor had begun as we were approaching the town. When I

told Joseph tonight was the night, he tensed up with urgency. We stopped by the inn, and Joseph spoke to the innkeeper. I was concentrating on my labor but sensed Joseph getting frantic as they turned us away. He begged desperately for someplace where we could have the baby, and we were finally directed to the stable, a cave in the hillside below the inn. We went down the path behind the inn, and there was the dark hole, warm with the breathing and bodies of the animals. Joseph borrowed a lamp from the inn and made a clear place with fresh straw in the depths of the cave. He built a fire outside and boiled water for me.

Elizabeth, we didn't even have time to find a midwife. I delivered the baby myself as Joseph waited outside. I was alone, yet not alone. The joy of the moment filled me with strength. This was God's child, and I felt God's presence surrounding me, surging within me with each contraction, making my labor a holy task.

Then the baby was born. After I cleaned up and wrapped him tightly in the cloths I had brought from Nazareth, I called Joseph in. He began to apologize; he felt he had failed me because we had ended up in such a place. I reminded him that this was God's baby and that if it was the will of the Lord for his Messiah to be born with the beasts of the stable, we must accept it.

So we lay down and looked at our baby—Jesus, "the Lord saves." The angel had told Joseph, "You shall call his name Jesus, for he will save his people from their sins." It's all so hard to believe. As I looked down at this tiny bundle nursing at my breast, it all seemed so ordinary. Wonderful, but ordinary. He is a baby like any other baby. He cries, he's helpless, he nurses, he sleeps just like every other baby born in the world. Oh, he's my baby, which makes him special to me, but who else cares? We are such poor folks from a poor town. We can't even find a decent place to spend the night. Our baby is born in a place where Joseph had to sweep out the manure. It's all so ordinary, even crude.

Yet there is something amazing going on. This little baby, so oblivious to everything except the warmth of my milk and the touch of my skin, is the center of some great cosmic drama. An angel was sent to me and to Joseph to tell us he would be born, that he would be the Son of the Most High God. He was conceived in my body, yet I had never lain with a man. When I visited you, John leapt within you as if in the presence of his Lord. You said I was blessed among women, and the Spirit of God filled me and gave me words of prophecy, words that are still awesome to me as I ponder them:

"My soul magnifies the Lord,
    and my spirit rejoices in God my Savior,
for he has looked with favor on the lowliness of his servant.
    Surely, from now on all generations will call me blessed;
for the Mighty One has done great things for me,
    and holy is his name."

Those things you know, but they were not the last of the wonders to be experienced.

Later that night we were awakened by visitors entering the stable. They were shepherds; they had come to see the baby! They had been taking care of their sheep in the fields when a numberless host of angels lit up the sky singing praises to God. One had told them a Savior had been born in Bethlehem, the Messiah, Christ the Lord. The angel said he would be found lying in a manger, which is where we had made a bed for Jesus. They had come to see and to worship. They fell on their knees, gazing at my sleeping little one. The oldest shepherd said a beautiful simple prayer of thanksgiving and blessing. They left so happy, talking excitedly about all they had seen that night.

When they had gone, I reflected on all they had said. Here was Jesus in the poverty of a smelly stable, and angels were ringing the praises of God across the skies. God was present—as the angel said, this was Emmanuel, "God with us." I wanted to laugh and cry, shout praise and be silent, all at the same time. It's like a glorious, wonderful joke. God has come as King, as Messiah, and he enters the world as an outcast in a stable. Who are his attendants? The wealthy nobles in their satin robes? No, the shepherds who smell of sweat and sheep. It is so gloriously funny. The Pharisees consider shepherding a despised trade, but the shepherds are the first guests invited to the Messiah's birthday party.

Dear Elizabeth, God has come among us, and it's not at all as we

expected. God is turning everything upside down. Remember what
the Spirit of God gave me to utter with you?

"His mercy is for those who fear him
from generation to generation.
He has shown strength with his arm;
he has scattered the proud in the thoughts of their hearts.
He has brought down the powerful from their thrones,
and lifted up the lowly;
he has filled the hungry with good things,
and sent the rich away empty.
He has helped his servant Israel,
in remembrance of his mercy,
according to the promise he made to our ancestors,
to Abraham and to his descendants forever."

That's what is happening with our little Jesus. He has come to
live with us in poverty and exile. He has invited the outcasts and
the ordinary to look in on his mysteries.

Once again God is upending the world, which has things all
backward in the first place. The world thrives on power, lusts after
wealth, glories in pomp and show. But God chooses the poor, the
humble, the downtrodden, the insignificant, and lifts us up to do his
will. So here is his Messiah, come to earth through me, a poor
peasant woman from Nazareth, wife of a struggling carpenter. Here
is his Messiah, helpless and homeless. Here is his Messiah, wor-
shiped by shepherds.

And hardly anyone else noticed that night. It was so easy to miss.
There were crowds all around us. They saw the new star shining
brightly in the sky but not the baby around back in the stable. They
were too busy. Too busy making money during this boom time. Too
busy cursing the inconveniences, cursing the Romans, scrambling
for the best places. Too busy living for themselves to notice the
wonder of God's coming among us. Perhaps God only comes to
those prepared to receive him.

It was such a strangely wonderful night that Jesus was born, but
a few days later a shadow was cast over my joy. We took the short
trip to Jerusalem to visit the temple and make the ritual purification
sacrifices after childbirth. We were greeted by an old man named

Simeon and an old woman, a prophetess named Anna. Perhaps Zechariah knows them, for they are regulars at temple worship. They both announced with great joy that Jesus was the promised one of God. Simeon's prayer as he held Jesus in his arms was so moving:

> "Master, now you are dismissing your servant in peace,
>   according to your word;
> for my eyes have seen your salvation,
>   which you have prepared in the presence of all peoples,
> a light for revelation to the Gentiles
>   and for glory to your people Israel."

Oh, the wonderful mystery, the prophecies of glory attending this child!

But then Simeon turned to me and said: "This child is destined for the falling and the rising of many in Israel, and to be a sign that will be opposed so that the inner thoughts of many will be revealed—and a sword will pierce your own soul too."

What did Simeon mean by that? A question arose to haunt me—what is this sword? My own soul shall know pain and sorrow over this child, yet is he not to be the Savior, the Messiah, God's promised one? The divine joke of the Messiah's being born in a stable now becomes more somber. The future of this child will perhaps be just as upside down as his birth. His destiny is glory and rule, yet his path is one of sorrow, a sorrow I, too, shall have to taste in its bitterness. The poverty of his birth is a sign of the continued burden Jesus will have to bear as God's promise unfolds in him. What that means is unclear to me now. I wait with fear and hope for the answer to my question, but for now I shall just enjoy him. The sword piercing my soul seems so distant as I hold this precious baby in my arms. Still he is not my child. He belongs to God. His is a purpose far beyond my imagining. I am blessed to be trusted with his care in these years of his childhood. I think I shall treasure them deeply.

Of course, we are not in the stable now. Joseph found a room for us to rent, and now that the census crush is over, I've gotten to like Bethlehem. We can live our lives without the gossip of the busybodies in Nazareth. Joseph is getting enough odd jobs in carpentry to keep bread on our table. I am feeling stronger every day and will be ready to travel soon. Perhaps I can come and visit you, and we can enjoy our babies together. Until then I am lovingly yours,

Mary

Preacher-to-Preacher Notes

How does a preacher do a first-person sermon across gender lines? I grappled with that question as I wanted to preach on Mary at a Christmas Eve candlelight service. Luke 2:19—"But Mary treasured all these words and pondered them in her heart"—was a wonderful invitation into the interior of Mary's mind and soul. The idea of doing a letter solved the gender problem. I did not have to act the part of a woman, but the letter artifice allowed me to speak as Mary. I could ponder with her what the meaning was of all that was going on.

My wife commented on how feminine the sermon was. I have her to thank for that. Both our marriage and the experience of going through childbirth twice with Sharon have provided opportunities to see dimensions of a woman's experience that would be critical in any story of Mary giving birth to Jesus. A woman could probably do a far better job than this, but then I invite women to find the ways to tell men's stories, too!

Folk songs are often told across gender lines. A male balladeer wishing to tell a woman's tale could start with a verse in which the singer meets a woman with a story to tell. The preacher can assume the role of a minor character in the drama, perhaps even a fictional character. But one must be careful that the dramatic device not get in the way of the truth of the biblical story or confuse the hearer about what really happened. Then we cross the line between preaching a first-person story and providing entertainment. The form and the dramatic artifices must always be secondary to the message. To paraphrase 1 Corinthians 13, if I have a great dramatic device for a wonderful sermon but don't have the gospel, I am a sounding brass or tinkling cymbal.

When I preached this sermon, I also incorporated into the service a reading from Luci Shaw's book of poetry, *Listen to the Green* (Wheaton, Ill.: Harold Shaw Publishers, 1971). The poem "Mary's Song" is written in a similar spirit, inviting wonder, seeking meaning, and coming in the end to the cross.

Zacchaeus:
Testimony of a Tax Man

TEXT: LUKE 19:1-10

He entered Jericho and was passing through it. A man was there named Zacchaeus; he was a chief tax collector and was rich. He was trying to see who Jesus was, but on account of the crowd he could not, because he was short in stature. So he ran ahead and climbed a sycamore tree to see him, because he was going to pass that way. When Jesus came to the place, he looked up and said to him, "Zacchaeus, hurry and come down; for I must stay at your house today." So he hurried down and was happy to welcome him. All who saw it began to grumble and said, "He has gone to be the guest of one who is a sinner." Zacchaeus stood there and said to the Lord, "Look, half of my possessions, Lord, I will give to the poor; and if I have defrauded anyone of anything, I will pay back four times as much." Then Jesus said to him, "Today salvation has come to this house, because he too is a son of Abraham. For the Son of Man came to seek out and to save the lost."

Hello, my name is Zacchaeus. My friends call me Zack, which is kind of nice because I didn't use to have many friends.

I live in Jericho, down near the Jordan River. It's quite a busy place because we've got these two major highways that run right through our town. We're a crossroad for trade and business.

Well, as you may know, the Roman Empire rules our country, and of course they want taxes from us. So I got a job as a tax collector and eventually worked my way to the top. I ended up as the chief tax collector for all of Jericho.

Let me tell you how I worked it. The Romans wanted a certain amount of money for their taxes, and they didn't care how I got it. So I would bill people for much more than the Romans wanted, send the Romans their share, and I pocketed the rest. Everyone in town knew what I was doing, but they were helpless to stop me. After all, I had the mighty Roman army to back me up!

As the head tax collector I had a lot of other guys working for me doing the same thing. And of course, I raked off a certain percentage of their profits, too. With all this money coming in, I was one of the wealthiest guys in town. I mean, I was loaded! I had a big, beautiful house, wore fancy clothes and expensive rings, and ate at the finest restaurants. You would think I had it made, wouldn't you?

But let me tell you, I was hurting deep down inside. I was so lonely you wouldn't believe it. Everyone in town hated me because they knew I was ripping them off. The only people I could even talk to were other tax collectors. We used to have parties all the time, bring in the local whores, get drunk. We were all trying to dull the pain of our loneliness, but it always returned to haunt us like some kind of ghost. It wasn't just the hangovers—something deeper left me aching. Nothing could fill that emptiness inside. Here I'd built up this big financial empire, and I felt as if my whole life was utterly worthless.

I don't know, but some of you may feel that way. You may not be as rich as I was, and you probably haven't stepped on as many people as I did, but you may be just as mixed up. If you're like me, you may feel lonely deep down because you are afraid to let anyone really know who you are. You're afraid nobody will love you and care for you if you let them see the garbage and hurt and fears that you secretly struggle with. Or you may feel that you need a sense of purpose, something worth living for. Your life has been going around in circles, and nothing you have tried has satisfied the longing you have to make sense out of life.

But I'll bet you have a lot of good defenses for those feelings. Some of you can put on a self-confident mask. "I can do it on my own; I'm tough. I can get along fine without anybody else." Some of you hide behind your sense of humor. You laugh a lot, keep things from getting too close to you by making your funny jokes. But I can hear the strain in your laughter because I was that way once. We laughed a lot at the parties at my house with all us tax collectors and whores.

Some of you even hide behind the church. You do a lot here and are active and involved, but you are afraid to let the power of God really get into your lives. You don't dare let other people in the church see any weakness or struggle in your life. You just smile, say "How are you? Oh, I'm fine!" and go your way.

I've used all those defenses myself, except hiding behind the church. You couldn't drag me into a house of worship with a team of chariot horses! But self-confidence, toughness, humor—I had those self-defenses up. Yet whatever I did, it never eased the deep longing I had for something more in my life.

Well, one day as I was sitting in my tax office, someone mentioned that Jesus of Nazareth was coming through town. I'd heard of Jesus before. He was a religious teacher who was kind of a renegade. The religious establishment was upset with him because he was always hanging out with the common folks and even with the really poor people. But what interested me the most was that I had heard he would actually talk with tax collectors.

Now no Jewish rabbi or priest in his right mind would talk with me because I had so much contact with the pagan Gentiles. That made me "unclean" in their eyes, and if they associated with me, they would be "unclean," too. So the religious folks didn't have much use for me, nor I for them.

But Jesus was different. I heard he would visit with tax collectors in their homes. I'd even heard that one of his closest disciples, a guy named Matthew, used to collect taxes up in Galilee.

So I had to check it out for myself. I left my office and headed toward the main road. When I got near the crowd, I could see it would be difficult even to get a glimpse of Jesus. He was surrounded by lots of folks who were crowding around to hear every word he might say. As you can see, I'm a little guy, so I didn't have much of a chance in that crowd. Besides, more than one person there wouldn't have minded giving me an accidental elbow in the throat! So I ran on ahead to a spot they would pass in a few minutes and climbed up this sycamore tree so I could see Jesus when he came along.

I didn't think about it at the time, but I must have been quite a sight. There I was, a grown man in these beautiful embroidered robes, with expensive rings on my fingers, up in a tree! I mean, really, now! But I just wanted to see this man who talked about God with people like me.

I'll never forget what happened next. Jesus came into sight, and then he stopped right by the tree I was sitting in. He looked up and peered right into my eyes. He just penetrated right through me, and I knew he could see all my hunger and hurt and desperation. But I wasn't afraid that he could see all that because there was so much love in his eyes. The love just poured out toward me.

Then he said my name: "Zacchaeus." He didn't spit it out like some foul cussword. I'd heard my name said like that a lot. No, he said it gently, but with a solid strength. He said it with a touch of pity and a lot of acceptance. "Zacchaeus"—I don't know how he knew my name, but he did.

Then he invited himself to my house for the night. I couldn't believe it! Jesus, a religious teacher, staying under my roof, eating dinner at my table! I almost fell out of the tree! And right then and there he left the stunned crowd and followed me to my house.

What an evening we had—just me and Jesus talking together! I knew Jesus could see what a mess I'd made of my life. He knew that I had mistreated people and that a lot of my wealth had been built up by extortion. But he didn't mention that at all. Instead he told me that God was like a shepherd who loses one of his sheep. And that shepherd will go out hunting all over the mountains to find his lost sheep, and when he's found it, he will invite his friends in and have a big celebration. God loves me like that. I was lost, and God went out to find me. Jesus wanted to bring me back to God and give me an abundant life. That's why Jesus wanted to come to my house. He came to offer me forgiveness for all the wrong I'd ever done. He came to offer me a new life, a new beginning, a life where

I could be at peace with God and with myself and with my fellow human beings.

And my friend, God makes the same offer to you as well. God loves you and longs to give you a new beginning in life. God will wipe away all the sin that you've ever done. God will take away the burden of your guilt and make you a new person. And don't think it's not possible. If God can love and forgive a guy like me, there's no problem loving and forgiving you!

But you know, if you open yourself up to that kind of love, it will change your whole life. Nothing will be the same again.

I knew I couldn't go back to being Zacchaeus the tax man, out to get every penny I could. No, if I was really going to have the new life Jesus offered, I would have to turn my back on what I once was and burn my bridges. After all, it would be rather foolish to take the forgiveness Jesus gave and then go back to the same empty, lonely, and mixed-up way of living I was trying to escape.

So I jumped up from the table and told Jesus I would give half of all I owned to the poor. After all, I certainly could live on a lot less, and I was beginning to see that Jesus loved those poor people too. I wanted to do something for all the people I'd cheated collecting their taxes. So I said I'd pay them back four times over to try to set things right. That wouldn't leave me with much, but it didn't matter anymore. I'd found something worth so much more than all my money and wealth.

Now, you may wonder why I would do such a crazy thing as that, and I'll tell you. I knew I had a choice to make. My life would either go Zack's way or Jesus' way. There really wasn't any in-between road. If I thought I could just be forgiven, get a pat on the head from God, but still continue in the kind of life I'd been living, I'd only be kidding myself. Jesus loved me, but I couldn't play any games with him. And I knew that his life was better than anything I could find on my own.

Well, each of you has that same choice: your way or Jesus' way. Don't think you can find the peace and joy that comes from following Jesus if you're holding back. He's got to be the Lord, the boss. He's the only way to having a really full and good life.

But if there's something from your old life that you can't let go, it's only going to hurt you in the end. With me it was my money and possessions, and I'm sure a lot of you would rather think about anything except what God may want of your wealth. But it could be something else you want to cling to. Maybe you are holding onto a grudge; you've let a wrong someone did to you poison your heart, and you just won't let it go. Maybe you are so tied up in your career that you are ignoring or even hurting people around you; you are a success, but what for? Maybe you are clinging to self-pity; you feel life has given you a raw deal, and you just wallow in your tears.

But, my friend, those things bind you and hold you back from the life Jesus wants to give you. So cut loose from them, give them up. Choose God's way. I did, and I've been a free man ever since. I've been at peace with myself. I've known a joy nobody can ever take away from me. And I'm not lonely anymore. Jesus said I was a child of God now, and it's true!

That's just the beginning of my story, but I hope it has spoken to you. Jesus Christ made me a whole new person, and he did it because he loves me. He loves you, too.

If you are here today and you've never opened yourself up to the love and forgiveness of Christ, then now's the time to do so. It doesn't matter how bad you feel about yourself or what you have done. Jesus loves you just as you are, and he wants to transform your life. And if you've got something you're holding back that you need to release, Jesus wants to help set you free. He wants to be your Savior and your Lord. He wants to forgive your sin and give you a new life to live. It's yours if you are willing to embrace it wholeheartedly.

Preacher-to-Preacher Notes

Because Zacchaeus was a tough guy who played fast and loose with ethics in order to get ahead, I envisioned him as a little on the unpolished side. Though he was wealthy, he had little sophistication. So I chose to use more idiomatic speech at some points. Since we can't use idiomatic forms of Aramaic in church—I certainly don't know Aramaic, and neither does my congregation—I used contemporary idioms. This may be less historically accurate, but I think it is more "character accurate." My point as a preacher is not to do pure history but to tell the story of God's work in human lives. So in this case I chose to modernize the language idiomatically to make the character emerge with the edge I thought Zacchaeus had in his own day.

With Zacchaeus's story I used a little humor to heighten the characterization, even though it was clear I was very different from him. I'm well over six feet tall, so when I came to the part of the story where Zacchaeus's stature is a key element, I said, "As you can see, I'm a little guy." As they could see, I wasn't! However, through my making that point explicitly with humor, we could all acknowledge the simultaneous realties of the preacher and the story character without any jarring effect.

Taking the first-person story in a totally different direction, I also wrote a rap version of the Zacchaeus story. My first church was in an inner-city neighborhood, with my office right on the main drag. In the summer I had the window up and would try to write sermons while periodically hearing the boom boxes blasting out their rhythms as people passed by. One day I decided not to fight the music as I worked with the message but to join it. The result was what follows. This was in the early days of rap before it hit the mainstream, but no rappers ever feared for job security because of me! I include this not because of its homiletical or artistic merit, or lack thereof, but to encourage you to tell the story any way it can be told.

Zack Rap

Zack is my name, tax collecting's my game,
    Folks think that I'm a dirty rat.
Wheelin' 'n dealin', cheatin' 'n stealin'
    In my job that's where it's at.
I work every day and my only pay
    Is what I can squeeze from you.
I take my share and a little to spare,
    There's not much left when I'm through.
Oh, you better watch out and you better not shout
    When I come passin' through.
I'm comin' your way, so you better pay,

'Cause, baby, your tax bill's due!
Yet deep inside I could have cried
'Cause I was messed up bad.
I had lots of things and diamond rings
But not a single friend I had.
Being alone is a real bad scene
Workin' 'n sleepin' 'n little between
There's gotta be more to get outta life
Than dollars 'n cents and grief 'n strife.
Glory, glory
I'll say it again now you join right in.

Glory (glory), glory (glory)
Wait till you hear the rest of my story.

One day in town I heard the news
Of Jesus Christ, the King of the Jews.
He ate with folks messed up like me
'N told them of a love that's free.
This Jesus was heading down Main Street
So I hustled and bustled and beat my feet
To the edge of a crowd all jammed in tight,
Pushin' 'n shovin' to see the sight.
Now I'm not tall, I'm kinda short
I just can't stretch up high,
So if I wanna see, I'd better climb a tree
Where Jesus might pass by.
I ran ahead, down the road I sped
Swung up on a low-hanging branch.
I got a box seat leanin' over the street
Then I waited for my big chance.

Glory (glory), glory (glory)
Wait till you hear the rest of my story!

Heads up, Zack, he's comin' your way!
Heads up, Zack, it's your lucky day!
I could now see him good and clear
The holy teacher was drawin' near.
He stopped before my sycamore
And looked up in the tree.
He saw me there hanging' in the air
And fixed a lovin' eye on me.

He said, "Zack, my man, come on down,
    Put your feet on some solid ground.
I've gotta have somethin' to eat tonight,
    So we'll go to your place, if that's all right.
I scrambled down quick as a wink,
    The folks in the crowd were makin' a stink:
"How could he eat with a bum like you,
    Such a friend would never do!"
But Jesus would have none of their talk,
    So he and I took a little walk.

Glory (glory), glory (glory)
    Wait till you hear the rest of my story!

We went on home and sat right down
    It didn't take long to get around
To the business at hand, namely, God and I,
    I was a sinner and about to die.
He told me that my soul was sick
    But Doctor Jesus could fix it quick.
I had to just admit my sin
    Trust in him and be born again.
He blew me away with what he had to say
    About God's love for me.
So I bowed my head, a prayer I said,
    And my poor heart was free.
Then I knew I had some work to do
    To put my wrongs all right.
I gave to the poor till I had no more
    And made their future bright.
It's no jive he made me come alive
    I follow him every day.
I'm feelin' fine, got peace of mind,
    'Cause I learned to trust and obey.
Zack's still my name, but now the Lord's my game
    I tell you I've been set free.
He set me straight t'ward heaven's gate
    I'm livin' like a brand new me!
So what about you? You know it's true
    God loves you just like me.
If you believe, you can receive
    His love that'll set you free.

Glory (glory), Glory (glory)
   That's just the start of my life story.
Glory (glory), glory (glory)
   Turn to Christ and you won't be sorry.
Yes, turn to Christ and you won't be sorry,
   Turn to Christ and you won't be sorry.

Naaman: The Healing of a Tough Soul

TEXT: 2 KINGS 5:1-19 (key verses: 8-14)

But when Elisha the man of God heard that the king of Israel had torn his clothes, he sent a message to the king, "Why have you torn your clothes? Let him come to me, that he may learn that there is a prophet in Israel." So Naaman came with his horses and chariots, and halted at the entrance of Elisha's house. Elisha sent a messenger to him, saying, "Go, wash in the Jordan seven times, and your flesh shall be restored and you shall be clean." But Naaman became angry and went away, saying, "I thought that for me he would surely come out, and stand and call on the name of the LORD his God, and would wave his hand over the spot, and cure the leprosy! Are not Abana and Pharpar, the rivers of Damascus, better than all the waters of Israel? Could I not wash in them, and be clean?" He turned and went away in a rage. But his servants approached and said to him, "Father, if the prophet had commanded you to do something difficult, would you not have done it? How much more, when all he said to you was, 'Wash, and be clean'?" So he went down and immersed himself seven times in the Jordan, according to the word of the man of God; his flesh was restored like the flesh of a young boy, and he was clean.

Greetings! I am Naaman. I lived 2,800 years ago in the nation of Syria, just to the north of Israel. My country seemed to be always at war with Israel. We fought constantly, and I was a commanding general. I was very successful, which brought me into the inner circle of our king, Ben-hadad II.

So I seemed to have a lot going for me. I was successful and powerful, but . . . I was a leper. There always seems to be a "but" in life, doesn't there? We may have all kinds of good things, but . . . My "but" was that I had leprosy. It was not the contagious variety, thank God. Poor souls with contagious leprosy were driven from society to live in hideous impoverished bands of outcasts. My type of leprosy was only a horrible nuisance. Whitish scales covered my body and made me ugly to look at. The condition was also physically irritating, which made me grouchy. Being ugly and grouchy was no problem for me as a soldier, but I hated living with this diseased body.

On one of our raids into Israel we captured an older girl, a young teen. I made her a slave to my wife. When she saw my condition, she said there was a prophet in Israel who had divine power. He could heal the sick. I talked to King Ben-hadad, and he gave me leave to go. I packed up gifts, money, and fine clothes and gathered a strong contingent of troops, and we all went off to Israel to look for this prophet.

First we went to the king of Israel; King Ben-hadad had written a letter instructing him to cure my leprosy. Most of the religious types were linked up with the government, so I assumed that the prophet of whom the slave girl had spoken was at the royal court. Civil religion isn't new; we had it back in my day. Well, the Israelite king got all upset. He thought we were trying to provoke a war, create some sort of insulting incident. He yelled in frustration, "How do you expect me to heal your leprosy!" Nobody could help us, or at least nobody *would* help us.

Somehow word got out from the court to the prophet Elisha, and he sent for me with a stinging rebuke to the Israelite king: "Let him come now to me, that he may know that there is a prophet in Israel." This Elisha was a very independent fellow. He followed God and didn't pledge blind allegiance and obedience to any king. So I left the royal court of Israel and headed out to where Elisha lived.

Now, there are many ways we try to bring healing into our lives, ways to deal with those "buts" I talked about earlier. I confess I was going about it all wrong; most of us do. We're so marred by our sin and woundedness that we try the wrong things to get ourselves on the right track. It's kind of like trying to put out a grease fire with water—you splash the burning grease all over and make the fire worse.

I first tried to buy my way to healing and wholeness. I had the money. I'd brought ten talents of silver and six thousand shekels of gold. That's tens of thousands of dollars in your money. I had the money and didn't mind losing all of it if I could get rid of this horrible skin disease. Elisha didn't accept it. He didn't even let me make an offer.

So often we think we are somebody because of what we have. Some people think they are special because they come to church with new clothes each week or because they put a lot in the offering plate. Or perhaps they think they are wonderful because they have given up so much to be good, clean-living, spiritual people. That's trying to buy off God, trying to buy God's approval—if not by flashing our money then by showing how important we are. It doesn't mean a thing. God totally ignores our strutting and posturing.

Those possessions and attitudes get in the way of our healing. They get in the way of our relationship with God. They come from our pride. If God paid attention to our pride, God would be just digging us deeper into the hole of our sin and brokenness, not helping us out. God's gifts aren't for sale. They don't go to the highest bidder, the flashiest dresser, the most sophisticated or most highly educated person—absolutely not!

Elisha completely ignored my effort to impress him with a gift of my wealth. Money can't buy healing. It may get the best doctors, but healing isn't for sale. Prestige can't buy healing. Power can't buy healing. God's healing is a gift. It's totally free. How it comes is a mystery. But however it comes, healing can be received only by those humble enough to take it, not by those of us who think we deserve it or can earn it.

So I was left with one more option, one more hope. I thought I could at least convince Elisha just to do his religious thing over me.

But Elisha wouldn't even come out of his house. He sent his servant with a message: "Go and wash in the Jordan River seven times, and your flesh will be restored, and you shall be clean."

"That's all? Wait a minute! Let's do something! I've come all the way from Damascus to see a prophet, so do your prophet stuff! Wave your hands, lay hands on me, say your healing liturgy, do a prayer service—do something!" I had a view of religion as some kind of magic; say a prayer, wave a hand—and presto!—everything's all okay.

We wish it would work that way, don't we? It would be nice if at the end of a service you could come forward, pray a prayer, and have your troubles fly away and your life be happy. But God isn't like one of those vending machines you modern people have. It's not a matter of finding the right combination of words or religious acts of devotion, pulling the right lever to get what you want. We think we can get God all figured out to act according to our plan. We can't heal ourselves, but God is supposed to be that big divine puppet that moves the way we want. Then when God doesn't perform on demand, we get angry.

I was furious. Who did Elisha think he was anyway? I wasn't going to take a dip in any Israelite mud hole of a river! We had sparkling waters in Syria; they would be far better, I thought.

How upset we get when we find God doesn't play our games. If God had given in to me, if Elisha had done things my way, I wouldn't have changed one bit. I might have been healed of my leprosy, but I'd still have been the same mean old cuss I was before. Though I was in desperate need, I still was expecting to have God submit to my desires and purposes, instead of submitting to God's purposes myself.

The way I was looking for healing was like a spoiled child demanding that the parent give in to its childish request. Who's in control around here? God is a good parent, so God withheld what I asked in order to meet my deepest need. God didn't play my game because God's desire was to heal me, to heal me in body and in spirit. But I couldn't see that yet, so I stormed off in a rage. I turned around all my men, my chariots, my cavalry, the pack train of treasure, and headed back home. "Forget you, Elisha. God's prophet! Hrumph!"

Ah, but my servants, God bless them! They started talking to me: "You want to get healed of your leprosy, don't you? That's what this trip is really all about, isn't it? You're willing to spend all this money. You'd be willing to climb the highest mountain or fight the hardest battle if we said that was what it would take. You would go through an elaborate ritual. So why not do the simple thing Elisha told you—go and dip in the Jordan River seven times?"

Why not? Yeah, why not? Maybe I should put aside all my plans, my assumptions, and try it God's way. What did I have to lose? Only my pride, my control, which got me nowhere . . . and my leprosy, which was the one thing I really wanted to lose.

So I went down to the Jordan River. "Dip in the Jordan seven times," the prophet had said. Simple, but not easy.

First I had to take off all my armor. That's not so bad, unless you're a leper. I had to expose my sores, my shame, my need. That's no easy thing. We spend so much time hiding our weaknesses from others, and even from ourselves. We build up defenses and deny the pain within us. The armor in our hearts is as solid as that iron breastplate that covered my own leprous body. I was shaking as I began to undo the catches and buckles that held my armor in place.

Healing can't begin until we strip ourselves and let the pain be seen. Once in the confusion of battle I was slashed by a spear across the palm. My instinct drove me to close my fist, to protect the wound. But I had to open the wound to get it washed and cleansed for healing. So it is with our deeper healing. I had to open up, bring my scaly, raw body into the open. We need to open ourselves up, face who we are, be honest and genuine. That's what confession is all about, my friends: honesty before God and even before our sisters and brothers. Through confession we overcome our pride, overcome our fear, overcome our shame, and let ourselves be known as who we are with our warts and weaknesses and wounds.

That's a scary thing to do. It's almost impossible to do alone. We need the support of caring people who show us acceptance and love. To confess is to become vulnerable. Your defenses are down; the armor is stripped off. But my servants and soldiers cared for me.

They wanted me healed. They were the ones who forced me to face myself and not run away.

And Elisha cared for me. At first I didn't think he cared because he didn't go along with what I wanted. But Elisha didn't want to ogle at my disease. He wanted to speak the word that led me to healing. When people around you are hurting, when they open up with their pains and diseases of body or soul, how do you treat them? Do you tenderly hold their vulnerable spirits in your hands with compassion and acceptance? I hope you do, for then you will be mightily used of God.

Now that I was stripped of all my armor, I got down in that old river and washed—seven times, and I was healed. The Jordan has no miracle waters; it's nothing special. It was God who healed. God's grace was extended toward me, toward a stubborn foreign leper.

What was important was that I trusted in God's word. I believed. Once I stripped off all my armor and protection, I was left only with the promise of the prophet. I would look ridiculous if it wasn't so. But that's faith. Faith is a risk, stepping out in trust that God's word is true. When God says believe on the Lord Jesus Christ and you shall be saved, faith says, "Amen! That's for me. I'll risk my life on that promise."

God puts forth the divine love and grace bluntly, simply: "There it is, my offer of mercy and forgiveness, my offer to make you a new creature, my offer to heal your inner self, my offer of abundant life, eternal life." But God always leaves us to perform the act of faith. It's up to us to follow through by trusting God's word.

You can take it, or you can leave it. Faith is taking it. Faith is going down to the river and washing in it. Faith is committing yourself to Christ again and again and again because you believe it is so—that true life and wholeness can be found only in him.

"Go, wash, and you shall be clean," the prophet said. It's in going and trusting what God says enough to act upon it that the healing process begins. Wholeness doesn't come instantly, particularly when we are talking about human nature. Healing of the body is easier than healing of the spirit.

I had to bathe seven times in the river. Sometimes it seems we go over the same territory again and again. We deal with the same problems, the same issues, the same frustrations. Life seems to be like running around an oval track: we're moving, we're going fast, but are we getting anywhere? The problem you once thought was solved creeps back in again.

Keep washing. Keep coming to the grace of Christ. Keep committing yourself anew to the Lord. God is at work, and that work of God is real. Your healing is taking hold. God has promised that it will be completed, and it will be.

The healing was completed in my body, but it was just beginning in my spirit. I was healed of my leprosy! My skin was soft like a baby's. It was not the tough, hardened skin of the warrior, the sunburnt skin of one who spends a lot of time outdoors. My skin was new, tender, completely healed, praise God!

That experience changed my whole life. I left the powerless, false gods of my old life and became a worshipper of the true and living God, the God introduced to me by Elisha. The One who had healed my body could now have my whole life and continue this mighty work of healing in my heart.

Because of what God did for me, because of the grace I experienced, I am confident that his grace will be sufficient for your own need. I am confident that grace will bring you to the healing and wholeness you desire. Come to God in openness and trust. Come and bathe in God's mercy. Come and take a dip in God's love. Come and take the first step in your journey of healing.

Preacher-to-Preacher Notes

The story of Naaman includes two additional twists. After he is healed, Naaman wants to give a gift to Elisha, but Elisha refuses. This is obviously different from Naaman's earlier effort to buy the healing. This is to be a thanksgiving offering, and Naaman offers it in honor of God. But Elisha still refuses to take the gift. (Perhaps this would make an interesting stewardship text!) Then Naaman asks for some soil from Israel, reflecting the common belief among the ancients that the gods were tied to particular geographic locations. By taking the soil back to his homeland, Naaman imagined that he was preserving the connection to God's "turf." His theology was inadequate, probably even to Elisha. He had not been saved by his theological correctness but by his willingness to act upon God's word through the prophet. Naaman goes on to ask permission to continue his duties with King Ben-hadad even when it will involve idolatry. Elisha gives him the blessing of God's peace.

This postscript to the healing story would make an interesting study in itself, but it would detract from the message of the sermon. A good story can have many layers and themes woven into it, but a good sermon needs to keep to its main focus with a few clearly related points. A Bible study would be a more appropriate place for spinning out the extra elements of the story.

The second major twist in the story is the greedy behavior of Elisha's servant Gehazi (featured in the next sermon in this book). Gehazi's greed has nothing to do with the healing plotline. But an interesting lesson might be found in comparing the views of money held by Naaman, Elisha, and Gehazi or in telling the whole story from Gehazi's vantage point. The story would then require a very different sermon form with a very different message. For Naaman, however, the Gehazi story is merely a minor footnote; it does not affect his own faith journey.

Gehazi:
Transforming the Traps

TEXT: 2 KINGS 6:8-23

Good morning! My name is Gehazi. Do any of you know who I am? I'm not one of the better-known characters in the Bible, but you've probably heard about the man I worked for: Elisha. I was the personal servant of the prophet Elisha and helped him in any way I could as he carried out his dynamic ministry in Israel.

Let me read a story from our lives that you can find in the Bible.

Once when the king of Aram was at war with Israel, he took counsel with his officers. He said, "At such and such a place shall be my camp." But the man of God sent word to the king of Israel, "Take care not to pass this place, because the Arameans are going down there." The king of Israel sent word to the place of which the man of God spoke. More than once or twice he warned such a place so that it was on the alert.

The mind of the king of Aram was greatly perturbed because of this; he called his officers and said to them, "Now tell me who among us sides with the king of Israel?" Then one of his officers said, "No one, my lord king. It is Elisha, the prophet in Israel, who tells the king of Israel the words that you speak in your bedchamber." He said, "Go and find where he is; I will send and seize him." He was told, "He is in Dothan." So he sent horses and chariots there and a great army; they came by night, and surrounded the city.

When an attendant of the man of God rose early in the morning and went out, an army with horses and chariots was all around the city. His servant said, "Alas, master! What shall we do?" He replied, "Do not be afraid, for there are more with us than there are with them." Then Elisha prayed: "O LORD, please open his eyes that he may see." So the LORD opened the eyes of the servant, and he saw; the mountain was full of horses and chariots of fire all around Elisha. When the Arameans came down against him, Elisha prayed to the LORD, and said, "Strike this people, please, with blindness." So he struck them with blindness as Elisha had asked. Elisha said to them, "This is not the way, and this is not the city; follow me, and I will bring you to the man whom you seek." And he led them to Samaria.

As soon as they entered Samaria, Elisha said, "O LORD, open the eyes of these men so that they may see." The LORD opened their eyes, and they saw that they were inside Samaria. When the king of Israel saw them he said to Elisha, "Father, shall I kill them? Shall I kill them?" He answered, "No! Did you capture with your sword and your bow those whom you want to kill? Set food and water before them so that they may eat and drink; and let them go to their master." So he prepared for them a great feast; after they ate and drank, he sent them on their way, and they went to their master. And the Arameans no longer came raiding into the land of Israel.

Did you catch me there? Not by name—I'm known in that story as "an attendant of the man of God." That's me.

It was an amazing experience, but it has a lot in common with experiences in your own life, at least for most of you. That may not be clear yet, but I hope it will be before I'm done.

So let me begin my story. Israel and Syria were at war a lot. Syria was our powerful neighbor to the north, always picking on us, harassing us. Elisha kept telling King Jehoram what the Syrians were up to. The king's army was able to escape from a number of ambushes as a result.

The king of Syria, Ben-hadad, started getting frustrated. "Why can't I pin Jehoram down? He seems to know my every move," he said. One of his counselors told Ben-hadad about Elisha, that his prophetic powers were Israel's secret defense. So Ben-hadad decided to get Elisha. He sent an army to Dothan, the city where we were staying at the time. He planned to seize and probably kill Elisha.

The Syrian army moved into position at night; we had no warning. I got up early the next morning and discovered that Dothan had been surrounded. Our soldiers were all excited and running around on the wall, getting ready for the assault. I went up on the wall and looked out. I saw the tents of the Syrian army spread across the countryside. There were chariots and horses. I could see the glint of spears and swords in the morning sun. We were outnumbered, out-armed, surrounded, trapped!

You probably know what it feels like to be trapped. You've been there before. Some of you may have experienced that in war, like I was facing, but for most of you you've been trapped in other settings. You may feel trapped in a bad marriage, trapped between a bad job and a pile of bills that won't let you quit or go looking for something better, trapped by discovering you're pregnant and not married or can't afford another mouth to feed, trapped by the clash of emotions within that seem too powerful for you to control, trapped by the illness within your own body—trapped! Your options are limited to bad and terrible, worse and worse still.

How do you feel in those situations? I felt afraid—scared of the horror coming, afraid of dying, particularly of getting hacked to bits. I felt helpless—I'm no hero; I'd look stupid swinging a sword. I felt confused—no time to think.

So I ran off to Elisha, "Oh, my master, what are we going to do?" It's nice to be able to dump all my fear, helplessness, and confusion on someone else. "You do something to get us out of this mess!" But we don't always have someone else. We can be very alone; we can be in the trap by ourselves.

At those moments we can be afraid of what the future holds. We can feel helpless at being unable to change the situation. We can be confused; changes are happening so fast that we can't sit down and think. We are under pressure to act and act NOW! Emotionally you can be bending like a tree branch. It can be bent quite a ways, but then suddenly it starts to crack and splinter. Something snaps inside ourselves—a nervous breakdown, illness from stress, beating on the kids, going on an eating binge, getting drunk, even attempting suicide. None of these actions solves the problem; we're still trapped. The Syrians were not about to go away just because I was upset!

As I said, when I saw the army, I scrambled down from the wall, rushed to the house where we were staying, and told Elisha what was happening. He got dressed and came out with me to the wall. In the face of my panic he was calm. In the face of my fear he was full of faith. In the face of my confusion he was assured.

He said, "Fear not, for those who are with us are more than those who are with them." This was patently false! The Syrians had a large army; we had only a few guards on the wall plus whoever in town could handle a sword or spear. We were hardly a match for professional soldiers.

But there was a critical assumption behind what Elisha said. He was assuming that there was more to reality than meets the eye. What you see is *not* what you get. You Americans have a card game called Black Jack where a player is dealt two cards. One card is face down, the other face up. The card that is face down holds the key to winning or losing. What you don't see makes all the difference.

The face-down card for us was God. Elisha knew that God was present with us, and that changed the whole balance of power. As King Hezekiah said a few years later when he was surrounded by the even larger army of Assyria, "Be strong and of good courage. Do not be afraid or dismayed before the king of Assyria and all the horde that is with him; for there is one greater with us than with him. With him is an arm of flesh; but with us is the LORD our God, to help us and to fight our battles" (2 Chronicles 32:7-8). The arm of the flesh is nothing compared to the arm of God.

But which of us can see the arm of God? I couldn't. I could see the Syrians. I could see their chariots, horses, and armed men. I could see our small detachment of guards. I could see the fear in their eyes. I could see the terror in the citizens of Dothan as they stashed away their valuables and prepared to hide or flee. But God? Where's God?

Elisha's confidence sounded like so much superficial hype to keep up our spirits—positive thinking so we would at least die hopeful! When you are trapped, faith-talk often sounds hollow and cheap. Can't they see the swords and spears? Hey, it's easy for you to talk. You don't have to pay six hundred dollars a month in rent and try to feed four kids on an income of five dollars an hour. You don't have to deal with the emotional wounds I've suffered. You don't have an alcoholic husband who beats you. You don't have a disease that debilitates you and is slowly killing you. You don't have a dark skin as a stigma in this racist society.

You don't have my problems, Elisha, so don't talk to me about those that are with us being more than those against us. Let's be realistic! We see the problems, we see the trap, but we are blind to the Lord, blind to the Savior.

Elisha prayed, "O Lord, I pray thee, open his eyes that he may see." He prayed for revelation, that God would show me what the situation really was. So often that is what we need. We need a touch on the eyes of our spirits so that we can perceive the presence of God.

So Elisha prayed, and suddenly I saw. All around us, spread across the mountainsides, surrounding the camp of the Syrians, dwarfing their army, was a stunning, brilliant host—the army of heaven! Angels, horses, chariots of fire! You sophisticated twentieth-century people may have a hard time believing this. You want to be able to document everything scientifically. There's no room for the supernatural, for mystery, or for God. But if God is real, there is more to reality than what is scientifically observed.

And angels are a part of God's creation, spiritual beings with power who can intervene in human history. They were present at the destruction of Sodom and Gomorrah. They announced the birth of Jesus and were at the tomb for his resurrection. And they spread across the hills of Israel to protect Elisha and the entire city of Dothan from the Syrian threat.

I believe in angels, for God opened my eyes to see what I couldn't accept in faith. My point is not to prove to you that angels are real. What is important is that God was present. I thought we were hopelessly trapped, but God revealed to me that the true situation was totally different. The Syrians were the ones in a trap!

God is also mightily present with you when you feel trapped. Centuries later the apostle John wrote something that sounds a lot like what Hezekiah had said: "the one who is in you is greater than the one who is in the world" (1 John 4:4). Christ is within you, the presence of God around you. That changes the cold, harsh analysis of so-called realism. God is stronger than any trap we feel stuck in. And I pray that you will know this truth in your heart—that you aren't alone, you aren't powerless, you aren't abandoned by God. God is present along with God's ministering servants, both angels and people.

Sometimes God's presence is seen in spectacular ways. Sometimes that presence comes in very ordinary ways, in the brother or sister who comes alongside to help. But when God reveals God's presence, the balance of power shifts. The Syrian army was no longer mighty. Our problems are no longer overwhelming. Our tragedies no longer have the last word. Our traps will no longer spring shut and crush us. We know by faith that God is with us, that God is our protector and deliverer. So the light of hope can dawn in our hearts where once only the gloom of impending defeat was known.

Once my eyes were opened, I was able to witness the most amazing end to a battle I've ever heard of. Elisha went out of the city, and as the Syrians rushed to seize him, they were all blinded. Elisha led this huge contingent of blind soldiers, each holding hands or touching shoulders, shuffling down the road, down the nine miles to Samaria, the capital city of Israel.

Once inside the great fortified city and before a stunned King Jehoram, Elisha prayed for them to see, and what a shock those Syrian soldiers got! *They* were surrounded by the army of Israel. The sandal was on the other foot now!

Jehoram asked what he should do with this enemy army delivered into his hands. Should he just butcher them? Instead Elisha told him to feed them, and that's what he did. Jehoram hosted a great feast for the enemy army, then let them return home—disarmed, of course. For many years after that the warring between our nations ceased. Now tell me, would any worldly strategist, any general or politician, be able to come up with an ending like that?

You see, when God is involved, anything can happen. When you feel trapped, it seems you have no options, or if you do have a choice, it's between the lesser of two evils. But God is infinitely creative. God can make a new option where nothing seemed to exist at all.

In fact, at the core of the Christian faith lies the most astounding breaking out of a trap ever, far greater than our deliverance at Dothan. Jesus was dead, brutally executed. His body was sealed in a tomb under armed guard. But what happened? He rose on Easter morning! Who ever would have dreamed of that! Nobody thought resurrection was an option. But God is a God of surprise. When everything seems hopeless, God can make a way. He parted the Red Sea to deliver Moses and the Israelites from Pharaoh's army. He delivered Daniel from the lions' den. He delivered Elisha and me from the Syrian army.

So look up! Take courage! Open yourselves to God's presence, and be ready for new doors to open, new options, surprises! God is able to heal your emotional scars. God is able to rebuild your fractured marriage. God is able to bring peace amid your stress. God is able to raise up your depressed spirit. God is able to empower powerless people. God is able to bring down injustice. God is able to weave peace between people. God is able!

The solution may not be instantaneous or easy. It may involve struggle, risk, crucifixion along the way. But the end is one of deliverance and victory, even of delightfully creative surprises.

May God's hope strengthen you all, for there is far more to our lives than meets the eye!

Preacher-to-Preacher Notes

A character like Gehazi can provide a vantage point for telling a story with another character as the central hero of faith. This story could be told through Elisha, but a listener would find Elisha a more difficult character with whom to identify. Most of us feel more often like the confused and fearful Gehazi than the confident Elisha in the face of severe threats. A character with an inner conflict also provides a better structure upon which to construct the story. Telling this story through Gehazi opens one up to the wonder of God's provision, whereas the story told through Elisha could easily slip into self-righteousness. Heroes who blow their own horns are not appealing. Gehazi's humility provides a better vehicle for gospel communication.

In many stories the storytelling preacher could invent a character, such as a person in the crowd watching Jesus or a dinner guest at the home of Simon the Pharisee when Jesus was present. The reactions of people witnessing the acts of God and the struggles of the heroes of faith are fairly accessible. We can put ourselves into those situations and feel the story through their perspective. Giving a name and a character to a person in the crowd allows the preacher to present specific feelings with which the listeners can identify. All of us in the contemporary church are onlookers to the biblical stories, so the shoes of the onlookers during the original event fit us well.

An alternative way to close this message would be to step back into the preacher's role immediately following the end of the story. Let Gehazi's question, "Would any worldly strategist, any general or politician, be able to come up with an ending like that?" stand as his conclusion. Take a step back; then step again into the pulpit commenting on how we can learn from Gehazi that when God is involved, anything can happen. Then finish with the rest of the text, revised to be spoken by the preacher.

Jonah, Part 1:
A Doomed Getaway

TEXT: JONAH 1:1–2:10

Now the word of the LORD came to Jonah son of Amittai, saying, "Go at once to Nineveh, that great city, and cry out against it; for their wickedness has come up before me." But Jonah set out to flee to Tarshish from the presence of the LORD. He went down to Joppa and found a ship going to Tarshish; so he paid his fare and went on board, to go with them to Tarshish, away from the presence of the LORD.

But the LORD hurled a great wind upon the sea, and such a mighty storm came upon the sea that the ship threatened to break up. Then the mariners were afraid, and each cried to his god. They threw the cargo that was in the ship into the sea, to lighten it for them. Jonah, meanwhile, had gone down into the hold of the ship and had lain down, and was fast asleep. The captain came and said to him, "What are you doing sound asleep? Get up, call on your god! Perhaps the god will spare us a thought so that we do not perish."

The sailors said to one another, "Come, let us cast lots, so that we may know on whose account this calamity has come upon us." So they cast lots, and the lot fell on Jonah. Then they said to him, "Tell us why this calamity has come upon us. What is your occupation? Where do you come from ? What is your country? And of what people are you?" "I am a Hebrew," he replied. "I worship the LORD, the God of heaven, who made the sea and the dry land." Then the men were even more afraid, and said to him, "What is this that you have done!" For the men knew that he was fleeing from the presence of the LORD, because he had told them so."

Then they said to him, "What shall we do to you, that the sea may quiet down for us?" For the sea was growing more and more tempestuous. He said to them, "Pick me up and throw me into the sea; then the sea will quiet down for you; for I know it is because of me that this great storm has come upon you." Nevertheless the men rowed hard to bring the ship back to land, but they could not, for the sea grew more and more stormy against them. Then they cried out to the LORD, "Please, O LORD, we pray, do not let us perish on account of this man's life. Do not make us guilty of innocent blood; for you, O LORD, have done as it pleased you." So they picked Jonah up and threw him into the sea; and the sea ceased from its raging. Then the men feared the LORD even more, and they offered a sacrifice to the LORD and made vows.

But the LORD provided a large fish to swallow up Jonah; and Jonah was in the belly of the fish three days and three nights.

Then Jonah prayed to the LORD his God from the belly of the fish, saying,

"I called to the LORD out of my distress,
    and he answered me;
out of the belly of Sheol I cried,
    and you heard my voice.
You cast me into the deep,
    into the heart of the seas,
    and the flood surrounded me;
all your waves and your billows
    passed over me.
Then I said, 'I am driven away
    from your sight;
how shall I look again
    upon your holy temple?'
The waters closed in over me;

the deep surrounded me;
weeds were wrapped around my head
   at the roots of the mountains.
I went down to the land
   whose bars closed upon me forever;
yet you brought up my life from the Pit,
   O LORD my God.
As my life was ebbing away,
   I remembered the LORD;
and my prayer came to you,
   into your holy temple.
Those who worship vain idols
   forsake their true loyalty.
But I with the voice of thanksgiving
   will sacrifice to you;
what I have vowed I will pay.
   Deliverence belongs to the LORD!"
Then the LORD spoke to the fish, and it spewed Jonah out
upon the dry land.

Good morning. My name is Jonah. I'm a prophet from the nation of Israel, and I lived over seven hundred years before the time of Jesus. I'd been doing the Lord's work for some time when the Lord spoke to me very clearly. He said, "Jonah, get up and go to Nineveh, that great city, and speak out against it; I am aware of how wicked its people are."

Now you have to realize that Nineveh was the capital city of Assyria, which was the mightiest military superpower of that time. Not only was Assyria powerful; it was our greatest enemy.

I didn't want to go. No way! I mean, the Assyrians were a terrifying people. They scared me. They had conquered many countries and often treated their captives brutally. What was a simple Jewish prophet like me going to do in the face of that awesome power and cruelty? No way, Lord! I'll be obedient, but only if you give me a decent assignment.

But I sensed God's guidance still before me: "Jonah, go to Nineveh!"

So I tried to get as far away as I could. I went down to the harbor

at Joppa and caught a ride on a ship headed for Tarshish, the place
you call Spain. That's on the other end of the Mediterranean Sea,
the last stop on the line. Maybe if I ran long enough and far enough,
God wouldn't hassle me. Besides, everything seemed to be fine so
far. All the doors were opening so I could run away from the Lord.
Maybe it didn't make any difference if I went my own way.

How often do you flee from the Lord just as I did? God lays down
something before you, but you want to avoid dealing with it, so you
run away. Some people will run away by going from place to place,
like I tried to do, or from job to job, or from spouse to spouse. You
can even run away from God within your own self. You can hide in
your own heart, just close yourself off from the voice of God. "I
don't want to change my life, God! I don't want to reach out and
forgive that person! I don't want to get involved in that situation.
Just leave me alone, God!"

But no matter how hard you try to run away, you can't escape
the presence of the Lord. King David wrote a psalm that says,

> Where can I go from your spirit?
>   Or where can I flee from your presence?
> If I ascend to heaven, you are there;
>   if I make my bed in Sheol, you are there.
> If I take the wings of the morning
>   and settle at the farthest limits of the sea,
> even there your hand shall lead me,
>   and your right hand shall hold me fast.
>   —Psalm 139:7-10

That's a great comfort, that God is there, a great comfort—unless
you're running away. You can run all you want, but you can't
escape. I know, because I tried.

I came to the end of the line a lot sooner than I expected to. While
we were at sea, a violent storm whipped up. The timbers of the ship
groaned and creaked as the waves smashed against them. It got so
bad that the crew even threw all the cargo overboard to lighten the
ship.

And do you know where I was while the storm raged? I was
down in the hold, sound asleep. Running away from the Lord
always leads to trouble, and that big storm was certainly trouble.

But I wanted to ignore the danger signals. I tried to sleep, hoping that everything would just blow over and that there would be sunny skies again. Don't we all do that sometimes? When a crisis is brewing in ourselves or in our families or in our communities, we can just pretend it's not there. Everything will calm down again—we hope. So we ignore the danger signals, and the situation just gets worse.

Finally, the sailors had to interrupt my slumber. "Hey, man, what are you doing sleeping? At least you can get up and pray that your god might save us!" How was I to pray to God? I was running away from God, so I shrank back into the corner and tried to make myself invisible.

Then the sailors cast lots—it's kind of like your games of flipping a coin or throwing dice. They cast lots to see who was responsible for this bad storm that had us all on the verge of a watery grave. And to my horror the lot fell to me. I was pointed out as the guilty one. I was running away, but now I couldn't hide it anymore. The sailors were desperate; the boat was beginning to break apart. What were they going to do?

So I resigned myself. God had me cornered. I'd thought I could run away, but now I was at a dead end. The least I could do was not drag down these other people with me, so I told the sailors to throw me overboard as a sacrifice to God.

At first they wouldn't do it, but the storm got even worse. So finally, with a prayer to God to hold them innocent, they heaved me over the side into the turbulent sea. This was the end, and what an awful way to go. I had run away, but I hadn't escaped.

Then, just as I was about to go under, a huge fish or whale or something rose out of the water and swallowed me whole. Curtains, I thought. A pretty dramatic way to come to the end of the line, I'll admit.

What does it take for you to come to the end of the line? What does God have to do to get you to stop running away? How can God shake you out of your spiritual slumber or your indifference or your rebellion? Sometimes it takes a tragedy, an awful loss in our lives to make us face the issue of what our lives truly count for. Sometimes it takes failure, seeing our dreams collapse around us. God doesn't necessarily cause such things, but they can be the brick walls we slam into as we are trying to get away from God.

I hope you won't have to go that far before really submitting to the will of God. But sometimes our stubbornness is so intense that God can't even get our attention. A crisis comes, and God tries to cut through all our defenses to open our minds and hearts to the divine will. The crisis shouldn't become a total disaster but rather a doorway back to the Lord.

Well, there I was in the smelly belly of this fish. I had a lot of time on my hands. There's not much to do inside a fish, let me tell you! So I did a lot of thinking.

At first I felt really lonely, cut off. God had performed a miracle to save my life by sending this fish to swallow me, but at first I didn't see it that way. Instead I felt that my agony was just being prolonged, stretched out with deliberate cruelty. I thought God had abandoned me. That's kind of funny because I was trying to run away from God, but when I finally thought I was out of his presence, I got upset—at him, for not being there. It's amazing how childish we can be, isn't it? We'll get mad at God for things that are our own fault. We turn our backs on the Lord and then get angry when we seem to be alone. How far we push God's patience!

Then as I sat around for a while inside that fish, I calmed down a bit. Gradually I began to sense that the Lord was with me. God was with me, but not like an arrogant victor who gloats over the loser of a game. God was there like the patient, loving parent of a disobedient child. It dawned on me that throughout the crisis God had been taking care of me, even if it meant preserving my life in the belly of this fish.

All at once a deep sadness over my own foolishness just welled up in me. I longed to receive God's forgiveness and love. I cried out to the Lord, "O God, here I am, I'm yours! I'm not much, but I'm yours." The Lord heard me and answered me. He flooded my soul with forgiveness and peace.

No matter how low you have sunk, how far you've run away, the Lord is right there to respond to your cry when you turn to him. God heard my cry in the belly of the fish. He heard the cry of David when he faced the guilt of his acts of adultery and murder. He heard the cry of the thief on the cross. He heard the cry of the woman caught in adultery. He heard the cry of the blind beggar, Bartimaeus. And God hears your cry. When you've come to the end of the line and can't run anymore, when you've faced up to your foolishness and cried out to the Lord for mercy, God will be there to embrace you, forgive you, love you, and remake your life.

At that point, thankful to the Lord for his mercy toward me, I renewed my commitment to him. As a prophet I had committed myself to obey him and to speak his word. Like Isaiah, I had received the call of the Lord: "Whom shall I send?" And I had answered, "Here am I; send me." Every one of you who has asked Jesus Christ to be your Savior has made that same kind of commitment. You've said, "Jesus is Lord, Lord of my life." That's a commitment to obey and follow wherever God leads. But like me, you too often fail to keep up your end of that commitment. You, too, don't always obey your Lord and God.

So I said to the Lord, "What I have vowed I will pay." I vowed obedience, so now I am renewing that vow. I will follow through on my commitment to you, even if that means going to Nineveh, going into the heart of the enemy's camp.

We all need to follow. We all need to be disciples of the Lord Jesus Christ. Not just talking about him. Not just gathering to worship and praise him. But obeying him. Following him into the heart of our hurting and rebellious world to proclaim God's words of mercy and peace. Following him into the midst of the injustice and violence of our world to do works of reconciliation and healing. Following him into the middle of that same world that crucified him, and being willing to face rejection and even crucifixion. Anything else is running away. Anything else is a dead end. But following the call of God is the only life that is worth it all in the end.

Well, after three days and nights that changed my life, the fish vomited me out near land. I splashed through the waves onto the beach, back home again. I was right where I'd begun, but I'd come a long, long way—a long, hard way. And I had changed. Now I was ready to follow, ready to obey, ready to be the person God wanted me to be.

Preacher-to-Preacher Notes

Many biblical texts assume geographical or historical knowledge on the part of the reader, but the contemporary preacher cannot make that assumption. So in telling the story we can unobtrusively insert the descriptive details that keep the listener in touch. In the Jonah story, for instance, all the Israelites would know that Joppa was a port city, but most of our church folks would have no clue where Joppa is. To refer to "the harbor at Joppa" provides geographical orientation without making a point about it. Such details make for both a richer story and more connected listeners.

Jonah, Part 2:
Obedience from the Heart

TEXT: JONAH 3:1–4:11

The word of the LORD came to Jonah a second time, saying, "Get up, go to Nineveh, that great city, and proclaim to it the message that I tell you." So Jonah set out and went to Nineveh, according to the word of the LORD. Now Nineveh was an exceedingly large city, a three days' walk across. Jonah began to go into the city, going a day's walk. And he cried out, "Forty days more, and Nineveh shall be overthrown!" And the people of Nineveh believed God; they proclaimed a fast, and everyone, great and small, put on sackcloth.

When the news reached the king of Nineveh, he rose from his throne, removed his robe, covered himself with sackcloth, and sat in ashes. Then he had a proclamation made in Nineveh: "By the decree of the king and his nobles: No human being or animal, no herd or flock, shall taste anything. They shall not feed, nor shall they drink water. Human beings and animals shall be covered with sackcloth, and they shall cry mightily to God. All shall turn from their evil ways and from the violence that is in their hands. Who knows? God may relent and change his mind; he may turn from his fierce anger, so that we do not perish."

When God saw what they did, how they turned from their evil ways, God changed his mind about the calamity that he had said he would bring upon them; and he did not do it.

But this was very displeasing to Jonah, and he became angry. He prayed to the LORD and said, "O LORD! Is not this what I said while I was still in my own country? That is why I fled to Tarshish at the beginning; for I knew that you are a gracious God and merciful, slow to anger, and abounding in steadfast love, and ready to relent from punishing. And now, O LORD, please take my life from me, for it is better for me to die than to live." And the LORD said, "Is it right for you to be angry?" Then Jonah went out of the city and sat down east of the city, and made a booth for himself there. He sat under it in the shade, waiting to see what would become of the city.

The LORD God appointed a bush, and made it come up over Jonah, to give shade over his head, to save him from his discomfort; so Jonah was very happy about the bush. But when dawn came up the next day, God appointed a worm that attacked the bush, so that it withered. When the sun rose, God prepared a sultry east wind, and the sun beat down on the head of Jonah so that he was faint and asked that he might die. He said, "It is better for me to die than to live."

But God said to Jonah, "Is it right for you to be angry about the bush?" And he said, "Yes, angry enough to die." Then the LORD said, "You are concerned about the bush, for which you did not labor and which you did not grow; it came into being in a night and perished in a night. And should I not be concerned about Nineveh, that great city, in which there are more than a hundred and twenty thousand persons who do not know their right hand from their left, and also many animals?"

For those of you who haven't met me, my name is Jonah. I'm a prophet from Israel who lived about seven hundred years before Jesus. Last week I shared with you my experience of running away from the Lord. I found I couldn't escape, no matter how hard I tried, so I finally yielded myself to him. When my journey in the fish was over, I was ready to obey God's leading, ready to follow. But I didn't realize that I still had a lot of growing to do.

When I got back home, the Lord laid his message on my heart again: "Jonah, go to Nineveh!" That was what God had said the first time when I ran away. Now God was giving me a second chance. This time I didn't hesitate. As soon as I could, I left on the long journey to Nineveh.

Nineveh was a huge city, and including its farmland and outlying villages, it took three days to walk across it. I traveled all about the various marketplaces and street corners, and everywhere I went I proclaimed a simple, blunt message: "In forty days Nineveh will be overthrown!" Their wickedness had grown to be so great that God couldn't tolerate it any longer. Sin must be punished. It inevitably leads to destruction, and the time was up for Nineveh.

But then something happened that I didn't expect. People took me seriously. From the most humble peasant to the mighty king, Nineveh was swept by revival. The king himself took the lead and called on everyone to repent, to turn aside from their violence and evil. Together the entire city turned to God in prayer. They realized that they didn't have any good deeds of their own to stand on. They had been corrupt and unjust and perverse. Their only hope was that God would be merciful if they turned to the Lord in humble repentance.

And, you know, God was merciful! In response to their repentance, God turned aside from the divine wrath. Though Nineveh had terrorized half the civilized world, though they were an incredibly violent society, when they turned to the Lord, God had mercy.

My message had been: "In forty days Nineveh will be overthrown!" But every word of judgment from God is conditional. You can always add the words "unless you repent" to the end of the message. If you turn aside from your wrongdoing, God will turn aside from his judgment. It's not that God's mind has changed, but you've changed in response to God's message. And since God is a merciful God, full of love and compassion, he immediately responds with grace to a sinner who turns toward him in repentance.

Now you would think a preaching prophet would rejoice over people turning to God, wouldn't you? But not me! God could forgive those people if he wanted, but I wasn't about to.

The people of Nineveh were my enemies. They had fought wars

with my nation and humiliated us by forcing our kings to pay them tribute. So I wanted to see them catch it! I wanted God to really do a number on them. I wanted fire to rain down from heaven upon them. The message of destruction was one I enjoyed bringing, and I wanted to see that warning carried out.

But God messed up my desire for vengeance, as I had known God would. So I gave God a piece of my mind. "God, I knew you would be an old softie. That's why I didn't want to come here. I want these people destroyed. I want to see them fry, and now you've used me to bring them to repentance! Well, I'm fed up, you hear! It's either them or me. If you want to spare their wretched lives, then why don't you kill me!"

Oh my, what a pout! I'd been obedient in proclaiming God's message, but I wasn't doing it from my heart. Just like a child who doesn't get her way will stomp off and pout in her room, I stormed out of Nineveh to a hill that overlooked the city and sat down. "God, I'm going to sit right here until you destroy that city."

Have you ever been angry with God because things don't go your way? Have you ever pouted or tried to force God to give you what you want? Well, if you have, you know exactly what I was trying to do. But the Lord left me with a question: "Do you do well to be angry, Jonah?" That's a question we always need to ask ourselves. When we get angry, are we letting our anger eat away at us and twist our spirits? Are we letting our anger close our minds to the will of God? Do we do well to be angry?

Now as I look back on that incident, I marvel at God's patience with me. God could have said, "Okay, Jonah, since you say you want to die if you don't get your way—ZAP!" But God didn't. God let me nurse my anger for a day as I sat under the hot sun, watching the city, waiting for the divine fire to fall.

Then during the night a large plant sprang up so that the next morning I was protected by its shade. It was obviously a gift from God, perhaps even a sign of blessing upon me as God's prophet. I started to feel pretty good, sitting there in the shade waiting for my enemies to be incinerated. Oh, how sweet were my thoughts of revenge!

But during the next night the Lord sent a worm or grub that bored into the stem of that plant. My shade shriveled up. "Hey, what's up, God? Are you playing games with me, killing off my little bit of shade?"

Then the Lord turned the tables on me and exposed my hatred, my anger, my self-righteousness and spiritual shallowness. "Jonah, you're all concerned about this plant, and yet you did nothing at all to bring it into being and make it grow. And now that it's gone, you pity it and are angry at its loss." Then God went a step further and drove the point home to this stubborn prophet: "Jonah, should I not pity Nineveh?"

The Lord had made all these people. Even though they had turned away from God and pursued all kinds of wickedness and violence, God had invested so much in them. God's love was deeply invested in the people of that city I hated so much.

In fact, God loves the whole world. You should know that better than I do because you now know about Jesus. You know that the Bible says, "For God so loved the world that he gave his only Son, so that everyone who believes in him may not perish but may have eternal life." You know that Jesus Christ died on the cross for the sins of all people, even those we dislike, even those who hurt us. Jesus died for those Roman soldiers who drove the spikes into his hands and feet. He died for Pontius Pilate and Herod, who sentenced him to death. He died for Judas, who betrayed him, and for Peter, who denied him. Jesus died because he loved them and wanted to free them from their bondage to sin and death. So if just one responds, if just one prodigal child returns home, if just one lost sheep is found, God rejoices and delights in pouring out the divine mercy. That's the nature of God's love.

Even though I lived before Jesus, I knew enough about God's love to know that God prefers mercy over judgment. The people of Nineveh repented of their wicked ways; now I had to repent of mine. I had to turn aside from the hardness of my own heart and learn to love the people of Nineveh. I had to learn to rejoice that they had been spared because they had turned to the Lord. If God loves them, so must I.

And so must you. You must love the Ninevites around you, the people who have hurt you, the people who have inspired your own

anger, hatred, and fear. You must purge the hatred from your own
heart with the compassion of our loving God. You must learn to
love your enemies whoever they may be: the one who breaks into
your home and steals your belongings, the one who cuts you off on
the expressway, the one whose shoddy work sets you up for the fall
at work, the liberals, the conservatives, the blacks, the whites, the
browns, the yellows. You name them; God loves them all, and so
must we.

Proclaim God's word—yes! Denounce evil—yes! But resort to
vengeance or malicious thoughts? No way, not as followers of a
God of love. We need to love the very ones that God loves and
rejoice over them when our enemies respond to that love.

The only way we can do that is to have God's heart. Do you have
God's heart in what you do, in how you relate to the people around
you? I didn't when I went to Nineveh. I preached God's word, but
I didn't have God's heart.

As religious people we find it very easy to have a form of
obedience to God on the outside, but not to have our heart in it.
When I was in the belly of the fish, I learned the importance of
obedience, but my heart wasn't in it. Oh, I was sincere while praying
in the belly of that fish, but that faded the closer I got to Nineveh.
I continued in obedience, but my heart wasn't in step with God's.
Obedience is important, but why do we obey the Lord? Do we do
what God says because we have to? If so, God's work within us is
not yet complete. That's why my story wasn't over once I had
finished the preaching mission in Nineveh.

God wants us to obey because we have his heart within us. God
wants us to identify with his concerns, his loves, his sorrows. I could
identify with God's concern over the evil of Nineveh, but I couldn't
share God's compassion that allowed him to be merciful when they
repented. My heart wasn't close enough to God's heart.

When we find ourselves in that condition, we need to enter into
the prayer that King David prayed when he was confronted with
his awful sins of adultery and murder. David prayed: "Create in me
a clean heart, O God, and put a new and right spirit within me"
(Psalm 51:10). David wanted God to transform his old, sinful heart
so that it became a mirror image of God's heart.

It's only with that kind of inner identification with God that we can fully obey—obey not just by our actions but with our whole selves; obey willingly, not with a complaining spirit; obey inwardly, not just outwardly. If we have opened our hearts to the Lord and to the love of God, then it comes much more naturally to obey God. As you know, Jesus said, "Those who love me will keep my word" (John 14:23). If you love God, obedience will begin to grow within you, growing from the inside out, growing from the heart into your actions. With God's heart, God's love within us, obedience comes ever more naturally. Our love for others, even for our enemies, is able to flow out because we have a source of love deeper than ourselves.

Being obedient from the heart—that's what I had to learn as the Lord showed me his love for the people of Nineveh. True, I had obeyed, but my heart hadn't been in it.

Where is your heart? Is it with the Lord and his work? Is it aching for those who are prisoners of sin, who are victims of injustice, who are swept away in violence, or who are seduced by delusions? Is your heart filled with compassion for the Ninevites of your day? If not, think on God's love for you. Think on God's love for them. Then go forth as a willing, obedient channel for that love to those who need it so desperately.

Preacher-to-Preacher Notes

In this sermon I have Jonah engaged in a running dialogue with God at a number of points. The dialogue with God can be easily set off from the address to the congregation by looking up and gesturing heavenward. Speaking to an imaginary character by facing a space—left, right, up, or down—conveys the dramatic shift of setting without the use of any extra words or props. The dramatist-preacher can move back and forth between the dialogue with another character and the storytelling to the congregation simply by shifting the line of vision and the tone of voice.

Should a character from the Old Testament ever refer to Jesus or quote from the New Testament, as Jonah does here and as Gehazi did in a previous sermon? You can make your own choice about that. Obviously, if one wanted to make a fully historical presentation, such references would be as inaccurate as a movie scene about the Civil War featuring a soldier with a Rolex watch. The detail may not affect the story, but it is historically out of place. Yet time has been transcended by the very relationship between the ancient character and the contemporary congregation. References to Jesus and the New Testament can be made if the character reflects that these come from the listeners' side of the relationship, not from the ancient character, thus preserving the integrity of the older dramatic figure.

In the story of Jonah the biblical text is very spare in telling about the plant and God's mercy for Nineveh. The points about love and compassion can be extended by drawing in the biblical witness from parts of Scripture Jonah never knew. This is one of the boundaries between drama and sermon where as a preacher I chose to put the emphasis on the sermon, though I was careful not to have too much of the sermon hang on material outside of Jonah's parameters.

Elijah: Listening to Voices

TEXT: 1 KINGS 19:1-18

Ahab told Jezebel all that Elijah had done, and how he had killed all the prophets with the sword. Then Jezebel sent a messenger to Elijah, saying, "So may the gods do to me, and more also, if I do not make your life like the life of one of them by this time tomorrow." Then he was afraid; he got up and fled for his life, and came to Beer-sheba, which belongs to Judah; he left his servant there.

But he himself went a day's journey into the wilderness, and came and sat down under a solitary broom tree. He asked that he might die: "It is enough; now, O LORD, take away my life, for I am no better than my ancestors." Then he lay down under the broom tree and fell asleep. Suddenly an angel touched him and said to him, "Get up and eat." He looked, and there at his head was a cake baked on hot stones, and a jar of water. He ate and drank, and lay down again. The angel of the LORD came a second time, touched him, and said, "Get up and eat, otherwise the journey will be too much for you." He got up, and ate and drank; then he went in the strength of that food forty days and forty nights to Horeb the mount of God. At that place he came to a cave, and spent the night there.

Then the word of the LORD came to him, saying, "What are you doing here, Elijah?" He answered, "I have been very zealous for the LORD, the God of hosts; for the Israelites have forsaken your covenant, thrown down your altars, and killed your prophets with the sword. I alone am left, and they are seeking my life, to take it away."

He said, "Go out and stand on the mountain before the
LORD, for the LORD is about to pass by." Now there was a
great wind, so strong that it was splitting mountains and
breaking rocks in pieces before the LORD, but the LORD
was not in the wind; and after the wind an earthquake,
but the LORD was not in the earthquake; and after the
earthquake a fire, but the LORD was not in the fire; and after
the fire a sound of sheer silence. When Elijah heard it, he
wrapped his face in his mantle and went out and stood at
the entrance of the cave. Then there came a voice to him
that said, "What are you doing here, Elijah?" He answered,
"I have been very zealous for the LORD, the God of hosts;
for the Israelites have forsaken your covenant, thrown
down your altars, and killed your prophets with the sword.
I alone am left, and they are seeking my life, to take it
away." Then the LORD said to him, "Go, return on your
way to the wilderness of Damascus; when you arrive,
you shall anoint Hazael as king over Aram. Also you shall
anoint Jehu son of Nimshi as king over Israel; and you shall
anoint Elisha son of Shaphat of Abel-meholah as prophet
in your place. Whoever escapes from the sword of Hazael,
Jehu shall kill; and whoever escapes from the sword of
Jehu, Elisha shall kill. Yet I will leave seven thousand in
Israel, all the knees that have not bowed to Baal, and every
mouth that has not kissed him."

I've preached sermons on Elijah these past two weeks. I've asked
him to speak to us himself for this final message of the series.

Good morning. Your pastor's sermons have been on my faithfulness to the Lord and my courage at Mount Carmel. You might say
that has been the upside of my life.

But there has been a downside. Just as I was met by the Lord on
Carmel's mountaintop, I was also met by the Lord in my valley of
despair. That's what I'd like to tell you about today.

It all began with Jezebel's threat to kill me. Queen Jezebel had
heard about the events on Mount Carmel. She heard how her patron
god, Baal, had been shown to be nothing at all and how I had ordered

the false prophets killed according to the Law. She was furious, and in her rage she ordered me to be found and killed.

I was filled with fear, with terror. Yes, I, Elijah, the mighty, bold prophet who had just faced down the king of Israel and his religious lackeys. I, Elijah, who had seen God's holy fire fall from heaven and light the water-drenched sacrifice. Here I was frightened, scared to death, and I took off for the wilderness like a wild rabbit.

How quickly our faith and feelings can flip-flop, go from strength to weakness, from mountaintop to a deep pit. Has such a turnaround ever happened to you? Have you ever felt strong in the Lord, only to stumble and fall the next moment? How frail our faith is, how feeble our determination to serve God, how fickle our loyalty to the Lord!

I fled into the wilderness, at a half-run all through the day. In the evening I came to a broom tree, a scrub tree that grows in the desert, about six or seven feet high. I crawled under the tree and was flooded with despair: "Lord, I've had enough! Take away my life! Let me lie down and die!"

Despair is a frightening feeling. It is more frightening than the violent anger of one like Jezebel, for despair is within. It comes from one's own soul. It leaves us feeling limp and powerless. My despair made me crawl under a broom tree and wait for the end to come.

Some of you have been there, under your own broom tree. Some of you may even be there now or perhaps are wrestling with those feelings. There are many paths besides mine to broom trees of despair: loss of a job, loss of a loved one, loss of health, death of a dream, death of a friendship, death of a cause, press of bills, demands of people, crush of one disaster after another. So many paths can lead to the broom tree where we lie down and say, "I've had enough! I can't take it anymore!" Some contemplate suicide; some drop out with drink, drugs, or television. Some live it up, attempting to drown their despair with pleasures, but inside they are dying and they know it. We are afraid, but we feel so helpless.

Then the angel came. God in gracious mercy sent an angel to me. The angel touched my prostrate body with gentle compassion: "Get up and eat." There by my head was a wheat cake and some water, nourishment for my body. This unexpected gift was also a sign of God's presence to nourish my soul. I slept and then ate again at the angel's bidding. I was sustained by that moment of ministry, strengthened enough to go on a forty-day journey through the desert. I wasn't strong, I wasn't whole, but I would survive. That grace and food, the gifts of God's angel, kept me going.

I believe God sends angels to each of us in our darkest hours. Maybe in the form of a brother or sister in the community of faith, someone who touches us, who nourishes our broken spirits or just holds up our heads to keep us afloat in the rising tides of despair. Don't turn aside from these angels; don't push them away. Maybe you can't rejoice over their gift yet, but you can still receive it. For here you will find the little bit of strength you need to press on, to survive in the wilderness through which you must go. Usually we still have a long journey ahead of us to get from despair to hope. Getting on the right track is not a snap, not an easy one-two-three process. It's a journey, a rugged one at times. We need sustaining grace to see it through. God sends us the needed grace, the ministering angels, so we can make it.

Sustained by the angel's gift, I came to Mount Horeb, also known as Mount Sinai. It is the place where God appeared to Moses and gave him the Law. Then I heard a voice: "What are you doing here, Elijah?" God had not led me here. There are times when God leads us into the wilderness. God led the children of Israel into the wilderness to shape them into a covenant people, a holy nation. You know about Jesus' being led to the wilderness for forty days. But I was in the wilderness because of my own fear, running away not to find God but to escape Jezebel.

"What are you doing here, Elijah?" That one question was enough to make me spill my guts to God. For forty days as I traveled, I churned and boiled inside. I thought of all I'd done for God, all my efforts, all my acts of faith. And where had they gotten me? On a wanted poster! I was the most wanted man in all Israel. Jezebel had a manhunt out to find me, dead or alive.

Oh, how we can churn and simmer inside ourselves, let our raw feelings have play to accuse and condemn God, accuse and condemn those who have wronged us, accuse and condemn even ourselves. The pressure builds. Like an infected boil, the pus of the spirit builds up; it built up in me. And God with that one question lanced my boil: "What are you doing here, Elijah?"

"You bloody well know what I'm doing here! I'm here because of you! I've put everything into being your prophet, and nobody cares. I'm the only one who worships you, and what has it got me? They're trying to kill me, God, and I'm wondering if you even care."

Have you ever wanted to make a speech like that to God? Well, I said those things, but they weren't all true. I had a rather slanted perspective. When God lanced my boil with his question, out came all the pus of self-pity, the pus of rage, the pus of resentment. But I wasn't honest about my own fear and unbelief and despair. I made no confession, only accusations.

Yet God in infinite grace took my accusations with gentleness. Sometimes we think we can't be honest with God about what we feel. We think we can't rage at God, tell God off, or even curse God. Maybe we think God is like so many of us humans, that God will respond immediately with rage and curses. But it's not so.

Many of the great people in the Bible questioned God in anger and confusion—David in the Psalms, Jeremiah, and Job. And now I had done the same thing, so I guess I was in good company. Did God blow us away for being so impudent as to question the Almighty One's wisdom? Did God smack us around for being out of line? Did God rain judgment down on our rebellious heads? No. God listened, let us blow off steam, then answered where appropriate. God affirmed God's own divine love for us and redirected us into the proper path. God can take it when you blow off steam in the divine presence. God won't turn away; rather, God will turn you back toward wholeness, understanding, and peace.

As I spouted off, God picked up on an underlying note: my loneliness. We prophets can fall prey to the temptation to think we are the only ones who are truly serving the Lord, and I fell to that temptation. "I, I alone, am left." I forgot about the hundred prophets that faithful Obadiah had hidden from Jezebel's murderous wrath. I forgot about my brother Micaiah who was as bold before King Ahab as I was. I forgot about the folks who were converted at Mount

Carmel. Instead I took my struggle into myself and was left cut off, alone with my fear and despair.

We are so susceptible to cutting ourselves off from one another just when we need each other the most. When we need an angel of mercy to touch us, a sister or brother with a shoulder to cry on, an arm to lean on, an ear to listen, a mouth to speak encouragement, a mind to give wisdom—at that very point of need we can so easily fall into the trap of a self-imposed shell. We suffer alone without the resources of love from the people of God. So there I was as the only guest at my pity party.

Then a voice said to me: "Go out and stand on the mountain before the LORD." And the Lord came to me. I was raw, open, hurting, and the Lord came to me.

But not as I expected. I was a thundering prophet in an age that needed a little thunder from God. So the wind came and split the rocks with its fury; an earthquake shook the ground; a fire roared around me. Was God going to give me my own medicine? But no, God wasn't in the wind, earthquake, or fire.

Finally, I heard a still, small voice out of the silence, a voice calling me: "Elijah. Elijah." God came to me in quietness and healing grace. Just as centuries after my time Jesus stood in a storm-tossed boat and said, "Peace, be still," and the wind and waves calmed down, so this gentle speaking of my name began to calm the tempest within my own heart. That still, small voice was saying, "Elijah, I know you. I know what is going on in your life. I know what's happening inside you. I know you, and you are mine."

God knows your name, my friends. God speaks to you in quietness if you will but listen. God says, "Be still and know that I am God." God says, "I know you, I love you, and you are mine." God speaks in our worship, in our brothers and sisters, in the recesses of our inner selves. Can you hear that still, small voice amid the silence? God is calling to you.

God asked me once more: "Elijah, what are you doing here?" Once more I said my piece. I used the exact words I'd spouted off before, but this time my heart was quieter. The feelings had been expressed in their raw power, and now I was quieter, calmer, ready to work on the real issues of my fear, confusion, and loneliness.

God listened and led me into the answers for my problems. When we let the Lord speak to us and calm our troubled minds and hearts, then we can get to work on the real issues: moving ahead, stepping out into the future, into our lives of struggle and ministry.

So God sent me out. "Go, return on your way," I was told. We who come into the presence of God are sent back into the ordinariness of life, renewed, recharged, and redirected. We can't stay with God on the mountaintop, just as we can't stay with our despair under the broom tree. We have to move on; God sends us out.

God gave me a specific task to do, actually three tasks. I was to anoint Hazael to be the next king of Syria, anoint Jehu to be the next king of Israel, and anoint Elisha to be my successor as prophet. I was to disciple Elisha and prepare him to lead when I was gone. There was work to be done, and how good it is when God's call is clear before us. We need to know the tasks God has given us, for they provide stability and direction; we know where we are going with our lives.

God also opened up my eyes to my brothers and sisters. "You're not the only one, Elijah. There are seven thousand others in Israel who are faithful to me." There was a community of faith I had ignored, and now God was giving me this community as a gift to sustain me in the days ahead. So I went away from my meeting with God with confidence and hope, knowing God's grace and God's gifts of call and community.

And you, my friends, wherever you are on your journey, know that God is there with you. Even in the darkness, even under the broom trees, even when your feelings boil within you, God is there. Open yourself to the divine presence. Allow God's grace to touch you. Let God speak to you in a still, small voice so that you may be sent on your way renewed, recharged, and redirected.

Preacher-to-Preacher Notes

This sermon, as I mentioned in its introduction, is the third of three I preached on Elijah. In the first two sermons Elijah comes off as the hero: the courageous figure who stands before the king to resist the prostitution of faith for the cause of the state and who challenges the false prophets of Baal on Mount Carmel. First-person sermons about such events, at least from Elijah's vantage point, can easily come across as conceited or pompous—we like our heroes modest, so they shouldn't blow their own trumpets. An effective first-person sermon could be done by a witness to these events, someone who was directly challenged by Elijah's message, someone in the crowd at Mount Carmel.

This story of Elijah fleeing into the wilderness gives an opportunity to explore the interior life of someone we tend to think of as strong and dominating. A first-person sermon allows the preacher to lay bare the soul of a person of faith torn by despair who finds grace at the end of the road. Speaking in the first person creates a safe place for the hearer to identify with the prophet and follow the journey to a point perhaps not yet reached.

A series of sermons on a character can also reach a proper climax in a first-person presentation. The preacher earlier presents the great testimony of faith of this prophet, but then we let Elijah in the first-person sermon reveal his own humanity. This makes our own heroism more attainable, for Elijah is not so unlike us, we discover.

Testimony of John Newton: A Sermon for All Saints' Day

TEXT: ROMANS 5:20-21

But law came in, with the result that the trespass multiplied; but where sin increased, grace abounded all the more, so that, just as sin exercised dominion in death, so grace might also exercise dominion through justification leading to eternal life through Jesus Christ our Lord.

As we observe All Saints' Day, allow me to introduce to you John Newton. He was an English pastor and hymn writer. We've been singing his hymns throughout the service today. I've asked him to tell us his story, so please welcome the Reverend John Newton into our pulpit this morning.

Good morning. I greet you in the name of our gracious Lord. The first truth you need to know about my life is that I was pardoned by grace. I was born in 1725 to a devout Christian mother. She died when I was seven. My father was a sea captain in the Mediterranean trade, and I went to sea at the ripe age of ten. By the age of fifteen I was completely on my own.

I was known for my "unsettled behavior and impatience of restraint." I was drafted by the Navy, then deserted, got caught, was stripped and flogged. The British Navy would trade troublesome sailors to merchant ships, so I was exchanged to an Africa-bound ship in the slave trade.

When we got to Sierra Leone, I jumped ship and worked for a white slaver named Mr. Clow. It was a disaster for me. He had a black common-law wife who hated me, and together they turned me into a slave for them. I was a slave who served their slaves. For a year I suffered at the bottom with poor clothing and no pay. I fell ill with a high fever and was denied food and water. Finally some other whites showed up, and Mr. Clow in shame set me free to work for them. Whether living as a slave myself or working in the slave trade, I was surrounded by misery and cruelty. And I took part in it.

I finally got a place on a ship back to England, the *Greyhound*. A violent storm arose on the sea and battered our ship. We suffered severe damage. Even though I was a veteran of the sea, I was so terrified by the raging of the storm that I felt I was doomed. I thought of my wicked life, looked at how I had lived, and concluded that my sins were too great to be forgiven. I was a doomed wretch heading for a watery grave.

But the ship survived its fearful ordeal, and with this sign of hope I cried out to God for mercy. "I began to know that there is a God who hears and answers prayers." As I confessed my sins and pled for mercy, I experience forgiveness and peace in my spirit.

> Amazing grace, how sweet the sound,
> That saved a wretch like me!
> I once was lost, but now am found,
> Was blind but now I see.
>
> 'Twas grace that taught my heart to fear,
> And grace my fears relieved.
> How precious did that grace appear
> The hour I first believed!

Sin abounded in my life, but God's grace abounded all the more.

I love seeing the response to Jesus in the Gospels of sinners who knew their condition. Tax collectors, harlots—they were the ones who responded so eagerly to our Lord. I can identify with them; that's exactly where I was.

It was the good people, the church people, who had a hard time with Jesus. They didn't know their need for grace, their need for pardon. Some of you have never sunk as low as I have, to the ugly wretchedness in which I lived. You think of yourselves as decent people. But don't compare yourself to John Newton, a corrupt young sailor; compare yourself to God's standard of holiness and righteousness. Then our hypocrisy comes to light; our arrogance, our pride, our selfishness, are seen for what they are.

God's Holy Spirit opens our eyes to our sin, convicts us of our need—our desperate need—for grace. This is not so that God can watch us grovel and be miserable but so that we are forced to face the problem. You can't treat a disease properly without making the correct diagnosis. Only when we see our sin can the treatment of God's grace be applied. Then the forgiveness that flows from Jesus upon the cross can be freely given to us. Then peace with God can be granted, for we have honestly faced God as the sinners we are and received his gracious pardon.

So at the age of twenty-three I became a Christian. I had been *pardoned* by grace. Now I would learn about being *purified* by grace.

John Newton, the Christian, went into slaving. I became the mate of a slave ship, and after that voyage I captained my own vessels: the *Duke of Argyle* for one voyage and the *African* for two. I commanded the ships that transported Africans in horribly inhuman conditions that resulted in scores of them dying on each voyage. I felt that this job was a gift of God's providence. It was viewed in my time as a decent, honest living. I thanked God for being led into an easy and creditable way of life. Nobody questioned slavery in those days except the slaves and a few Quakers we all considered eccentric anyway.

But grace was at work to purify me. At first I felt it was my duty as a Christian slave-ship captain to treat the blacks under my care with as much decency as possible, within the limits of safety. Black slaves outnumbered the white crew six to one, so we kept them in chains in the hold at all times. Ships had been destroyed by slave revolts when the crews relaxed their vigilance. I tried to be decent within that situation, but it was impossible. The Holy Spirit began to prod my heart and my human sensibilities. I began to see the suffering of the men, the women, and the children in those wretched holds. The tension between my faith and my profession made me more and more uncomfortable, but I didn't know what to do about it.

Finally I had to leave the sea, not because of courage of conviction but because of a violent illness. Thus I was spared any more work in this iniquitous trade. But I was merely at the point of having an uneasy conscience. Grace was once again teaching my heart to fear.

I got a job as a clerk in an office and began studying Greek and Hebrew in my spare time. At the age of thirty-nine I was ordained in the Church of England, and I went on to pastor the church in Olney for sixteen years. While I was pastoring in Olney, I had contact with John Wesley, George Whitfield, and the powerful evangelical movement that stirred the country under their leadership. Wesley was one of the first to raise biblical concerns over the slave trade, and I became convinced it was an evil that needed to be abolished.

I wrote a pamphlet, "Thoughts upon the African Slave Trade." In it I attacked not only the evil of being personally involved but also the evil of our whole society in having a part in the commerce of human beings. I wrote,

> The best human policy is that which is connected with a reverential regard to Almighty God, the supreme governor of the earth. Every plan, which aims at the welfare of a nation, in defiance of his authority and laws, however apparently wise, will prove to be essentially defective, and, if persisted in, ruinous. The righteous Lord loveth righteousness, and he has engaged to plead the cause and vindicate the wrongs of the oppressed. It is righteousness that exalteth a nation; and wickedness is the present reproach, and will, sooner or later, unless repentance intervene, prove the ruin of any people.

I concluded the treatise, "Though unwilling to give offense to a single person, in such a cause, I ought not to be afraid of offending many, by declaring the truth. If, indeed, there can be many, whom even interest can prevail upon to contradict the common sense of mankind, by pleading for a commerce so iniquitous, so cruel, so oppressive, so destructive, as the African Slave Trade!"

In 1790 I became pastor of St. Mary Woolnoth in London. Crowds of people came to the church, including a young politician named William Wilberforce. To God be the praise, I was able to direct Mr. Wilberforce into the Abolitionist movement, and he it was who led the fight in Parliament finally to ban slavery throughout the British Empire.

God's grace continued to operate throughout my Christian life, convicting me ever more strongly of something I had first thought of as decent and showing me the utter wickedness of it. "I hope it will always be a subject of humiliating reflection to me, that I was once an active instrument in a business at which my heart now shudders." But yet again, where sin increased, there grace abounded all the more. God had mercy on me and purified my life of this evil.

How often, even for Christians, sin can be so close to us, so accepted as the normal way of operating, that we don't even see it for what it is! In fact, I've seen Christians justify, endorse, and quote the Bible in support of something completely alien to the spirit of the gospel. It happened in my day, and it is happening in yours. We can be so blind to our own sin, especially social sin that everyone around us accepts.

It takes a courageous openness to allow the Spirit to convict us. As the psalmist prayed, so should we: "Search me, O God, and know my heart: try me, and know my thoughts: And see if there be any wicked way in me, and lead me in the way everlasting" (Psalm 139:23-24, KJV). Such examination of the soul is not easy to do; it was not easy for me.

Our whole identity can be wrapped up in that wrongdoing. Slaving was once my job, my life, and I even believed it was a gift of God to me. To hear the voice of the Spirit was to turn my back on so much I had once seen as good. But it wasn't good; it was evil. So just as the Scriptures say, I had to crucify myself. "I am crucified with Christ: nevertheless I live; yet not I, but Christ liveth in me: and the life which I now live in the flesh I live by the faith of the Son of God, who loved me, and gave himself for me" (Galatians 2:20, KJV).

We can receive a new life in Christ. We can grow in that new life by letting Christ live in us. His grace unfolds progressively, bit by bit, day by day. We keep turning up sins that need forgiveness and repentance. But the more I discover of my need, the more I discover of his sufficiency, the more I discover of his amazing grace.

I was pardoned by grace. I was purified by grace. And so I proclaimed grace. I preached the gospel of our Lord Jesus Christ for forty-three years. I preached not as a righteous man but as a sinner who found God's grace in his hour of need. I feel a lot like the apostle Paul when he said, "This is a faithful saying, and worthy of all acceptation, that Christ Jesus came into the world to save sinners; of whom I am chief. Howbeit for this cause I obtained mercy, that in me first Jesus Christ might shew forth all longsuffering, for a pattern to them which should hereafter believe on him to life everlasting" (1 Timothy 1:15-16, KJV). If God could have mercy on me and transform me, he can touch anyone.

Even as an old man I said, "Shall the old African blasphemer stop while he can speak?" Perhaps the obituary I wrote for my gravestone says it all: "John Newton, Clerk. Once an infidel and libertine, a servant of slaves in Africa, was by the rich mercy of our Lord and Savior Jesus Christ, Preserved, Restored and Pardoned, and Appointed to Preach the Faith he had long labored to destroy." I *had* to tell about this glorious God.

But God also gave me a gift with poetry and music. As a sailor I used to make up rhymes and songs ridiculing the ship's officers. I would get the whole crew singing these mocking tunes. But God's grace turned this gift toward writing words of praise and edification. I took my love for Jesus, my experience of God's grace, and put it into music for all God's people to lift up in praise.

I worked with a famous poet in our congregation at Olney, William Cowper. Together we published *Olney Hymns,* which contained 280 hymns I had written, along with many from Mr. Cowper. Most have been long forgotten, but I see some are still used to express your praise to the Lord today. I am humbly grateful to have been so used by God.

You have known grace in your lives, too. So proclaim it! Bear witness to that amazing grace! I had gifts of preaching and music to proclaim God's grace. Your gifts may be similar; they may be very different. But use your skills; use your gifts whatever they may be to honor God and to make known his grace. Share your faith that others may discover new life in Christ. For God's grace is sweet and powerful.

How sweet the Name of Jesus sounds
In a believer's ear!
It soothes our sorrows, heals our wounds,
And drives away our fear.
It makes the wounded spirit whole,
And calms the troubled breast;
'Tis manna to the hungry soul,
And to the weary rest.

So proclaim that sweet name of Jesus. Tell of his grace. For the sake of our God, for the sake of our world, for the sake of this old slaver who found mercy and all those like me who haven't found it yet—tell it!

Preacher-to-Preacher Notes

I've often used All Saints' Day as an opportunity to preach from the lives of various people throughout church history. This provides an annual opportunity to instruct people about our heritage of faith. If the issues of that particular historical era can be made to come alive, they can speak to us as we seek to live faithfully amid the contemporary issues of faith and ethics.

John Newton's story was an adventure for me. I'd heard the tale of the writer of "Amazing Grace" who had once been a slave-ship captain in many a sermon illustration. During my research in our local public library, however, I stumbled across an old copy of Newton's "Thoughts upon the African Slave Trade" with a biographical introduction. There I discovered some twists to the story that had been lost through the emphasis on personal salvation testimonies.

I learned that he captained the slave ships *after* he had become a Christian, not before. That completely changed the story! Then as his social conscience was awakened, he moved into speaking prophetically and seeking political change. It was astonishing to me that the pastoral connection between Newton and Wilberforce had not been a highlight of the testimonies I'd heard. Newton's story, as I now knew it in its fullness, told us that just "getting everybody saved" was not enough to change society. The converted had to apply gospel faith to matters of justice, for God cares for those who are beaten down by the structures of oppression. Newton realized this and moved from an unquestioning piety that was comfortable with injustice to a prophetic activism against the greatest social evil of his day. His pastoral and prophetic guidance of Wilberforce affected the course of history. The sermon I thought I was doing was completely transformed by the historical figure I encountered.

Besides hearing Newton's voice in the first-person sermon, the congregation heard his words in all the music used in the worship service. Of course, "Amazing Grace" had to be sung. We also could choose from "Safely through Another Week," "May the Grace of Christ Our Savior," "Glorious Things of Thee Are Spoken," "How Sweet the Name of Jesus Sounds," and "Come, My Soul, Thy Suit Prepare."

When in the character of John Newton I quoted the Bible, I used the King James Version, the text he knew and used. I tried to use language forms a bit more akin to the style of his time. Often I used his very words, whether taken from hymns or from his writings. In the sermon text Newton's actual words appear within quotation marks.

Epilogue:
The Heart of the Matter

There is a profound difference between a drama and a sermon. Dramas are creations of human artists which at their best reflect aspects of our humanity so that we can see ourselves afresh. We may laugh at our foibles or be shaken by the evils of which we are capable, but through the dramatic arts we are addressed in our humanity by other humans.

In a sermon we are also addressed by another human. But that man or woman is also speaking "the word of God," however we might understand that phrase theologically. As Christians we understand an additional dimension of communication to be woven through this human interaction: God is present; God is speaking. The preacher's words may not be fully adequate or accurate, but God uses them directly to address a human heart. God's word is proclaimed through the preached word uttered by human mouths.

None of us called to the preaching ministry is adequate to the task. We have our narrow interests, our pet issues, our particular experiences that color our interpretation. We have limitations of skill, knowledge, and language. But God still chooses to use human vehicles for communicating the saving word.

My mother-in-law gave me an ordination gift that I keep on my desk and upon which I frequently reflect. It is a small square clay pot with a plaque on it that reads: II COR. 4:5-7. The passage to which it refers reads:

> For we do not proclaim ourselves; we proclaim Jesus Christ as Lord and ourselves as your slaves for Jesus' sake. For it is the God who said, "Let light shine out of darkness," who has shone

in our hearts to give the light of the knowledge of the glory of God in the face of Jesus Christ. But we have this treasure in clay jars, so that it may be made clear that this extraordinary power belongs to God and does not come from us.

We are "earthen vessels," as the old King James Version puts it. The treasure is the knowledge of the glory of God in the face of Jesus Christ. We speak, we use our skill, but all our homiletical skill is just an ordinary container for the extraordinary gospel that can transform human lives.

In approaching a first-person sermon, then, in researching, writing, practicing, and preaching it, I as the preacher need to keep in mind that it is ultimately God's word that I bear. It is not my word. I am not the treasure, merely the vessel for delivering the treasure to those who need it. For a dramatic sermon I especially need to remember that my evocative skills, my eloquent words, and my passionate presentation aren't the key elements. Good drama can contain all these qualities. Good preaching needs to carry yet another element that is not mine to own or control.

The critical element for good preaching is the anointing of the Holy Spirit. That is true for any sermon. In a first-person sermon the Holy Spirit is the director of the drama. The Spirit was at work in the initial drama in the human life of the particular character. The Spirit was at work in the writing down of that drama in the words of Scripture. The Holy Spirit continues to work in taking those words and making them come alive for people today, sometimes through the presentation of a preacher.

The practical side of this theological affirmation is that we need to bathe in prayer all we do in our sermon preparation and delivery. We pray to center ourselves around the treasure of the knowledge of God in Jesus Christ. We pray to offer ourselves as channels for the work of the Spirit. We pray to listen to the Spirit's word to us, that we might be addressed before we seek to address others. We pray for the direction in our choice of format and words so that the sermon may carry God's message to those who hear. We pray for the work of the Spirit within the hearts of the listeners so that God's word may be fruitful in their lives.

The tools of the dramatist can often be very manipulative.

Screenwriters know how to craft a touching moment at the end of a film to bring a tear to the eye and a catch in the throat. Both before and after the time of Sinclair Lewis's fictional portrayal, real-life Elmer Gantrys have appeared with regularity in religious circles, using their skills to sway crowds and raise big offerings. Any good speaker or storyteller can learn how to play the game. But cynical manipulation of dramatic tools is alien to the Spirit of Christ. The Spirit moves people's hearts and may use dramatic forms to do so, but God seeks responses drawn out of understanding, honesty, freedom, and trust. The apostle Paul brought integrity to his preaching: "We refuse to practice cunning or to falsify God's word; but by the open statement of the truth we commend ourselves to the conscience of everyone in the sight of God" (2 Corinthians 4:2). The manipulative cunning we could use with our dramatic skills must be purged from our hearts so that our skills can become Spirit-anointed gifts for building up the Body of Christ.

First-person sermons pick up a part of God's old, old story related in the Scriptures. We tell part of that story, the shorter story of a particular individual or incident. The ancient story enters into the present moment of the hearers in the congregation, coming alive with contemporary vividness. But then the preacher fades away, and the main character in the overarching story, the living God, continues the divine work of salvation, liberation, and healing in the lives of the people. Our sermons are delivered, but God takes those words and works with them. The Spirit convicts, consoles, confronts, and counsels. The Spirit goes far beyond where any preacher can go to remake an individual's life from the core of his or her being. God's story goes on with new chapters ever unfolding. The old, old story still shapes the new, new stories being written in men and women today.